ON TIME AND ETERNITY

Other New London Librarium titles by
Rubem Alves

The Best Chronicles of Rubem Alves

Tender Returns

*Art of Love: Paintings by Colleen Hennessy,
Thoughts from Rubem Alves*

Pensamentos: Bits of Wisdom from Rubem Alves

Concerto for Body and Soul

ON TIME AND ETERNITY

RUBEM ALVES

translated by
Glenn Alan Cheney

New London Librarium

On Time and Eternity
by Rubem Alves
Original Title: *Sobre o Tempo e a Eternidade*
Translated by Glenn Alan Cheney

Copyright © Glenn Alan Cheney 2020

Published by
New London Librarium
Hanover, CT 06350
NLLibrarium.com

All rights reserved. No part of this book may be duplicated in any form whatsoever without the express permission of New London Librarium or the translator.

ISBNs
Hardcover: 978-1-947074-43-9
Paperback: 978-1-947074-42-2
eBook: 978-1-947074-44-6

for Raquel

Contents

Time

Childhood

Fisheye	15
The Baptism	21

Adolescence

A Gift for the Mother of a Teen	29
On Birds and Adolescents	33
The Revolutionaries are Coming	37
The Crowd	43
To the (Possible) Thrushes	47

Maturity

Soufflé Time	55
On Male Sexuality (I)	59
On Male Sexuality (II)	65
For a Son	71

Old Age

Old Age	79
Miguilim's Eyes	85
The Useless Tree	91

Eternity

Wisdom

The Secret Garden	101
Illness	107
Mental Health	111
The Rat Gnawed the King's Cheese	117
The Gift	123
I Did Not Travel	129
It's in Talking that We Misunderstand	135
Sad Song	141

Love

To Lovers, with Care…	149
Tenderness	155
Violins Don't Grow Old	161
Maps	167
Abelard and Heloise	171

Eternity

The Happiness of Parents	177
The Egg	181
Cadavers	187
I Want a Yellow Ribbon…	191
For Tom Jobim	195
The Final Agreement	201
Odyssey	205
Rio	211

Gratitude	217
Rubem Alves	218
The Translator	219

Time

I

Childhood

Fisheye

I have believed in the Amazon River since I was a boy. My father was the first to tell me about it. He said it was so wide that you couldn't see the other side. I, who was used to fishing for minnows in creeks and streams, heard him say that the largest river he'd ever seen, the Grande, would be a little boy's pee compared to the Amazon. At school, I memorized and recited the names of tributaries that had been fashioned into a poem: Juruá, Tefé, Purus, Madeira, Tapajós, Xingu. I also learned about the pororoca[1], the battle that the river alway loses because the sea is greater than it. That's how life is: the sea always has the last word. But what fascinated me even more was the news about a water lily leaf so big that a child can lie down on it. It was all astonishing.

I believed in it without ever seeing it, just hearing about it. I believed in the river so much that I actually went there to see it. When one goes, it's because one has believed. And I saw the river with my

---

[1] The pororoca is a tidal wave that sweeps up the Amazon during new and full moons. The wave can be up to 12 feet high and travel 500 miles inland.

own eyes. And when I want to see it again, I re-read a poem by Heládio Brito:

> *I came to see the river*
> *the languid flow of the waters,*
> *weighted down by themselves,*
> *swollen from coming so far*
> *in the course of being river.*
> *Tired ox liquid*
> *loaded down with fish,*
> *the river works*
> *for the men on the banks,*
> *who with sweated backs flog it*
> *with their hooks and nets.*

I even got to navigate its waters, if crossing on a ferry is navigating. No, no it isn't. Whoever sails with their head above the water doesn't know anything. You have to dive under, penetrate deep into the waters. But to do so, we would need to be like fish. Guimarães Rosa loved rivers so much that he wished to be born a crocodile in another incarnation. We humans know rivers only at the surface. Crocodiles know them in their depths. In their depths, rivers are dark and calm, like the sufferings of mankind. That was something I did not know, that sufferings are dark and calm...

And then he said something unexpected: that *river* is a magic word for conjuring eternity. I had learned the opposite, that river is a word for "everything flows, nothing is permanent, all is a river..."

But reading Scripture, I noticed that John was right: "Eternity lives at the bottom of the waters, at the bottom of time." When God wanted to perform magic tricks on Jonas, he threw him into the sea, where a fish awaited him with open mouth, and for three days he stayed in the depths of the waters, like a fetus in a mother's belly, until he turned into a prophet. Which isn't much different from the metamorphoses a poet goes through—a portent confirmed by Cecília Meireles and T.S. Eliot, who affirm that, to create poetry, you must have the eyes of a fish. So it isn't just by chance that the magic ritual for the transformation of an old person into a child, to which we give the word "baptism," follows the metaphor of drowning and birth: the adult is submerged, full body, in the water of a river. The old one who submerges dies. The creature who comes out of the water is a child.

So it isn't by chance that the fish was, a while ago, a poetic symbol and prophetic symbol: that it swims in the depths of time, where eternity gives birth to its miracles.

On the surface of the river is the time that flows without stopping. That's how it was written on the old grandfather clocks, those enormous timepieces with pendulums in no hurry: *tempus fugit*—time flies, life goes on losing itself in the waters of the nevermore. All that's left, then, is longing without cure, if there had been love and joy. The big bash at the end of time is justified only if there had been no love, no happiness. The loss of something loved cannot be feted. It can only be lamented.

But as I thought about what the poets and prophets say, I found myself turning tears into smiles. Those who sow tears shall reap happiness, for God is the river showing his insides. At the bottom, in eternity, waters run the other way, as the fish that swim against the current know. As the soul knows: on the surface, people are born as babies, *tempus fugit*, and people turn into adults, *tempus fugit*, and we get old, *tempus fugit* and we die. In the depths, where eternity lives, it's the opposite. First it's old age. Then *tempus fugit*, and we turn into children.

God always begins at the end. In the Scripture, the day begins with afternoon and ends in the morning. It's written in the poem of the Creation: "And it was on the afternoon and the morning of the first day..." The sun sets, but a new day begins. The end is the place of beginning.

When we recite the seasons of the year, we automatically say: spring, summer, autumn, winter. But when I read D. Miguel de Unamuno, I saw that this was not right. Time is a wheel. If in the Scriptures the day begins with the afternoon, in the year, seasons may very well begin with winter. Winter, spring, summer, autumn... Winter is the childhood of the year. In its deep silence, spring is in gestation... In the silence of the end reside beginnings. In the silence of old age lives childhood...

There are people who firmly believe in God in the same way that I believe in the Amazon River, by hearing about it—then expounding on it with authority, invoking theology and dogma, like my father, who taught me about the Amazon without ever going there or seeing it. God doesn't sink himself into it in fear of drowning. Now I believe in God like a crocodile or a fish for me to un-drown. I need God for time to go backwards. And that's how I imagine it, like a fisherman who goes casting his nets of eternity across the waters of time to catch everything he loved and lost. It's spring being born out of winter. It's the child being born from old age.

That's what I wish for in the new year: children born from the old, that I be more of a child than I was.

The Baptism

My son Sérgio made a strange request. He asked me to plan a rite of baptism for Mariana, my granddaughter. I told him that to go through with that rite, it was necessary to believe. I don't believe. For many years the words of priests and pastors have been empty for me, even though I continue to be fascinated by the beauty of the Christian symbols as long as they are contemplated in silence.

He didn't give up, and he argued: "But you did my wedding..." Yes. I remember how he "put in his order" for the ritual: "Dad, don't speak the words of religion! Just speak the words of poetry!" And that is the way it went. They were the words of "The Canticle of Canticles," an erotic poem from the Bible that makes devout men and women blush. "Your two breasts are like the twins of a gazelle! (...) Your lips drip sweetness like honeycomb, and beneath your tongue, milk and nectar are found." I enjoy thinking about the face the pope and bishops would make if they read those words. They were followed by words of Drummond, Vinícius, Adélia[2]—all ending not with the annoying "Marcha Nupcial" ["Nuptial March"] but with Chico's "Valsinha,"[3] when the guests, young and old, grabbed their partners and set themselves to dancing. It was beautiful. When something is beautiful, we believe it easily.

So I remembered a passage from Alex Haley's *Roots* where he describes the name-giving ritual for newborns in an African tribe.

> Omoro (the father) then walked out before all the assembled people of the village. Moving to his wife's side, he lifted up the infant and, as all watched, whispered three times into his son's ear the name he had chosen for him. It was the first time the name had ever been spoken as the child's name, for Omoro's people felt that each human being should be the first to know who he was. They beat drums. Omoro whispered the same name in his wife's ear, and she smiled with pleasure. Then it was the whole village's turn: "The name of the first son of Omoro and Binta Kinte is Kunta!" After the full ritual, Omoro, carrying little Kunta in his strong arms, walked to the edge of the village, lifted his baby with his face to the heavens, and said softly, "Fend kil-

---

[2] Adélia Luzia Prado Freitas (b. 1935), Brazilian poet and writer who wrote about Catholicism and the body.

[3] Chico Buarque de Hollands, (b. 1944), Brazilian composer, singer, dramatist, poet whose performances and recordings of the 1960-1970s criticized the military government and also celebrated romance, as the song "Valsinha" (Little Waltz) did.

ing dorong leh warrata ke iteh tee." (Behold the only thing greater than yourself!)

This memory convinced me, and I tried to make up a name-giving ritual, since none that I knew of satisfied me.

I organized the space in the living room. I pushed the low coffee table toward the fireplace. At the head of the room I set an old bench. There Mariana would sit. To the side, two chairs—one for the father, the other for the mother. At the end of the table, a large candle. It's Mariana's candle, a candle that had been with her for her whole life and which had to be lit on all her birthdays. To the side of the candle, two long, colored candles. And, scattered throughout the room, candles of all types and colors. At the edge of the table, beside Mariana's candle, a wooden dish with a bunch of grapes.

Once all the guests were assembled, the ritual began. This is what I said: "Mariana, we are here to tell you the story of your name. It all began in great darkness." The lights went out as we heard the sound of Jean-Pierre Rampal's flute.

"Thus was your mother's belly, a dark, calm and silent place. There you lived for nine months. Once that time had passed, you tired and said, "I want to see light!" Your mother heard your plea and did as you wished. She gave you to the light. You were born."

Mariana's mother and father then lit the big candle, which shined alone in the middle of the room.

"Just look what happened! Your light has filled the room with joy. All the faces are smiling at you. And because of that joy, each one of them will also light their candle."

With that the godmother and godfather lit the long, colored candles, and the others lit, one by one, all of the candles around the room.

When the guests had arrived, I gave each one of them a little card where they were to write their deepest wishes for Mariana. I continued:

"You brought such joy that each one of us wrote on a little card a good wish for you. So, take this basket. Go to each one and collect the good wishes that they have written. These little notes, you will keep them for the rest of your life..."

And Mariana went around with the basket and her big blue eyes, from person to person, being blessed by them all.

"Everyone has given you something good," I said after the cards were collected. "Now it is time for you to give everyone something good. You are as plump and sweet as a grape. That is the purpose of this bunch of grapes. This is what you are going to do. Your godparents are going to make a little chair, and you, seated there, will give each one of them a piece of yourself, one sweet, plump grape.

And so, slowly, without knowing it, Mariana celebrated this unusual eucharist. "This sweet, plump grape is my body..."

When the eucharist was over, I said to Mariana:

"Now, coming to the end, each one of us is going to say your name. Pay good attention. The name is just one. But each one will say it with a different music. Because there are many different ways that you are loved."

And so, illuminated by the candles, each one of those present, looking deep into the girl's eyes, said, "Mariana," "Mariana," "Mariana," "Mariana."

Those who looked into Mariana's eyes could see that, as she heard her name being repeated, they filled with tears...

II

Adolescence

A Gift for the Mother of a Teen

Dear Mother: If I had the power to honor you on television, I would do something very simple. Just a silent image, perhaps Michelangelo's *Pietà*, or Picasso's *Mother Nursing a Child*, or one of Vermeer's paintings, *Woman in Blue Reading a Letter*. Just the image with the word "motherhood." You would feel more lovely, finding yourself beautiful in the imagination of artists.

But nothing like that gets done. You must be tired of seeing the ways television insults you, that its advertising describes you as a vulgar and hollow. "We have everything to make your mother happy," says the idiot announcer from a chain of stores. A woman whose happiness is the same as that of a kitchen appliance? What cheap happiness. It's bought with a blender, a microwave oven, a hair dryer. Another ad says "Don't forget Mothers Day. Because mothers remember."

I was thinking about that when I decided to give the mothers of adolescents the greatest of all possible gifts. I know how much the mothers and fathers of teenagers suffer. Often they come to me with a request: "Please, help us resolve our son's problem!"

So this is my gift: based on long experience, I want to declare that you have no problems whatsoever. Forget about them. They do not exist. It's all imagination. Sleep well!

You think I'm kidding? I have never spoken so seriously. What is a problem? Imagine you are knitting. All of a sudden the yarn gets tangled up in a knot. You can't knit with the yarn all bunched up. That's what a problem is—something that disturbs or impedes a course of action. But that's not all of it. What characterizes a problem is the possibility of a solution. You know that, with astuteness and patience, you can undo the knot. If there's no solution, there's no problem.

It's nighttime. You are preparing to knit. Then you find out the dog has chewed up one of your knitting needles and run off with it. Now you only have one needle. There's no way to knit with just one needle. Your action was interrupted, but you don't have a problem because, more so than you think, there is no way to knit with just one hand. So you put the yarn aside and go do something else.

That's how it is with adolescence. It isn't a problem for the simple reason that, as much as you think, there is no solution.

So I am going to give you two definitive pieces of advice to guide your adolescent son or daughter.

First: don't do anything. Don't try to do anything. Everything you do will always be wrong. Don't get mixed up in it. Don't say anything. Don't advise.

This may seem totally irresponsible. Parents' love says that they should try, to the limits of their strength, to help their children. I agree. It's just that there are situations where, if you try to help, you mess things up. Jay W. Forrester, professor of administration at Massachusetts Institute of Technology, stated a law for organizations that says "In complicated situations, efforts to improve things often tend to make them worse, sometimes a lot worse, in certain situations turning them calamitous." I imagine that the professor discovered this law while trying to guide his teenage kid. Because that's exactly what happens.

Many centuries ago, Taoism came to the same conclusion. There in its sacred book, the *Tao Te Ching*, it says "the fool does things without stopping, and everything is left to do. The wise man does nothing so that everything that should be done is done." For Taoism, the supreme expression of wisdom is to restrain yourself from the temptation to do. Don't do. Just look from afar. Life has its own wisdom. Anyone trying to help a butterfly from its cocoon will kill it. Anyone who tries to help a sprout come out of a seed will destroy it. There are certain things that have to happen from the inside out.

That's really so, because if you still haven't grasped it, the adolescent isn't interested in doing the right thing. He or she is interested in doing *his or her* thing. Now, if you tell the teen what is reasonable, that reasonableness will go on to be a mom or dad thing. To do the right thing, then, is to confess to a condition of dependence and inferiority, which is unthinkable and intolerable to a teen. The teen will then feel obliged to do the opposite.

I remember a mother of an adolescent of 13 years who was lamenting, "The alternatives were clear. On the one hand, a good option—rational and reasonable. On the other, complete idiocy. I explained everything to her perfectly right. Know what she did? She chose the idiocy. Why?" And I answered her, "Because you told her what was reasonable. If you had said nothing, there would be the possibility that she would choose one of the two alternatives. At the moment you said that your option was the first option, she was obliged to opt for the second."

Second: stay close to pull the broken pieces together. The pieces, when not fatal, can have an educational effect. Fact is, it's not worth getting upset over, staying awake and getting anxious. These states of being will in no way change the course of things. The adolescent is an entity that has escaped your control.

The illusion that something can be done leaves us anxious because we don't know what that thing is. The moment when you notice that there's nothing to be done, calm returns. Then you are free to do things. Don't let the craziness of your adolescent take control of you. Go see a movie. Go walk around with your husband. Show the teens that they don't have the power to ruin your life. Don't pointlessly miss a night of sleep. Remember that kids at a crazy party don't even remember that you exist. Sleep well. Happy Mother's Day.

On Birds and Adolescents

If the Sphinx had been just a little smarter, a little more versed in the mysteries that would be revealed only centuries later, instead of asking Oedipus that silly riddle, it would have simply asked, "What is more mysterious than the Holy Trinity and more painful than Christ's cross?" Of course Oedipus would not have been able to solve such a terrible enigma, and the Sphinx would have gone on to devour him, which could have saved us from the Oedipus complex and its postscripts in psychoanalysis. If he had been the mother or father of a teenager, the answer would have jumped right out: "It's my son, it's my son…"

Still, even though I know it is not possible to decipher such an obscure enigma, in pure compassion with desperate parents, I accept the painful duty of revealing what I have learned on the subject.

In the first place, it's important not to confuse things and to understand that there are two types of adolescence.

The first of them is a benign illness that seems like measles: the "age of adolescence." It's a time of life that generally goes from 13 to

19 years of age. This kind of adolescence has always existed. We all go through it. It's an individual phenomenon, normally healing on its own and rarely leaving effects. It is characterized by physical and psychological transformations. The voice changes, hair appears in the appropriate places, sexual organs develop, and figurines and dolls are traded for more interesting toys.

There's a second kind of adolescence, one that seems more like small pox in its severity. It's a modern cultural phenomenon of an essentially collective nature and characterized by a disturbance in the thought process, a loss of contact with reality, psychotic hallucinations that often take the form of social daring, as in the case of graffiti on walls and monuments, even high speed car races that often end up at funeral homes.

Behavioral psychology, initiated by Pavlov and developed by Skinner, has given an inestimable contribution to the study of human behavior, showing that it is possible to understand man through the study of animals. Dogs, guinea pigs, and mice were and are widely used for that purpose. Nevertheless, one thing I know is that no animal has been found that is good for the study of adolescence, which explains the dearth of knowledge in that area.

For many years I was reluctant to make my revolutionary discovery public. I remembered Darwin, who was cruelly hounded and ridiculed for having revealed our simian ancestry. I was afraid of suffering retaliation if I revealed that the enigma of adolescence can be deciphered if we study the social and psychological behavior of parrots...

Yes, parrots. Even under superficial examination, the similarities jump out at us.

To start with, parrots and teenagers always go around in flocks. A parrot alone and an adolescent alone are aberrations in nature. Thus the horror adolescents have of staying home. At home, they are separated from their flocks. Having cut the umbilical cord that had connected them to their parents, they replace it with another umbilical, the wire of the telephone through which they are permanently connected with one another. They can't stay alone because it makes them feel cold.

And parrots are all the same. And so are adolescents. Have you ever seen a teen at a party dressed differently from everyone else? Sneakers have to be of a certain brand. Jeans by the same designer. The party is a temple where adolescents celebrate their sameness.

Thrushes don't suffer identity crises. They are solitary birds, which is why they sing so beautifully that they could make one weep. When they sing, everybody shuts up and listens. Parrots are the opposite. They all scream at the same time. God save anyone (he hasn't saved me) from sitting next to a table of teenagers at a Pizza Hut. They all say the same thing, say it the same way, say it without stopping. But they don't notice because nobody's listening.

And, finally, parrots and adolescents don't care what direction they're going. They do care about the "flap" they raise while going.

But that's not all. At some future time I will reveal things even more shocking. I hope that you have noticed that the essence of what I'm saying can be summed up thus: in situations where crying is useless, all we can do is laugh. Until, of course, there are pieces to pick up...

The Revolutionaries are Coming

Some psychologists said to be specialists in adolescence advise, as a remedy for the disturbances characteristic of that phase, a lot of dialog, a lot of love, a lot of understanding. Parents should create conditions that let their kids talk with them about their problems, and that they should make an effort to understand them. Through love and dialog, they guarantee, parents and teens continue to be friends, and the family will go back to being as happy as they had always been when the teens were tots.

I disagree. In the first place, nothing convinces me that adolescents are after their parents' love. After love, yes. But their parents? Doubtful. In the second place, there is nothing teens want less than to be understood by old people. In arguments between husband and wife, there is a moment when one of the two says, as a final argument, "I understand you very well..." —an affirmation always made with a certain pause and a sneering smile. It's a way of saying, "Stop lying. I have you figured out inside my head. I can see through you. I've already done a CAT scan of your soul...Anything you say will be futile. I understand you. I have already solved your mystery." To understand is to dominate.

And do you really believe that adolescents want to be understood by their parents, those big cast iron balls the kids have to drag around, chained to their ankles, parents the teens still have to depend on so disgracefully for money and car, who watch over them like the eye of God and who ask for explanations of where they've been and what they've done, beings who can be escaped only at the price of lies and trickery? What prey wishes to be understood by a hunter? If the hunter understands the prey, it will know where to set the trap.

The hunter needs to understand the prey without depending on the good will of the prey to have a discussion. And the understanding begins when one realizes that the teen is still mentally a child; the only difference is the size of the body. And that's what makes all the difference.

Understanding children is easy. All you have to do is read the tantalizing comic strips about Calvin, which appear every day in Section C of the *Correio Popular*, that prestigious newspaper. (All newspapers need to be referred to as "prestigious" the same way that the pope is his holiness, the president his excellency, and the dean his magnificence.)

A child's head is dominated by fantasy, by wonder: Calvin is an astronaut, his mother is a tractor, a bicycle has its own ideas and acts on them. He's an incredible modern sculptor who makes amazing sculptures of snow. For absolutely logical reasons, 6+5=6, and the stupid teacher marked it wrong on the test. In the head of a child, everything is possible.

"Buy it, daddy? Buy it!"

"But I don't have any money," the father responds, lying.

But the child counter-attacks. "Pay with a check."

In the old days, fairies used magic wands. Now they use checkbooks.

Children think adults are omnipotent. When I am in a full elevator and I see a small child on the floor, splayed out in the middle of the adults, I imagine what the kid's seeing when she looks up—enormous towers. I think it was from similar situations that fantasies of giants were born, giants who eat children. For children, adults are giants of uncommon strength who can do anything.

If Calvin had power, if he were big and had a checkbook, the world would be totally different—all toys and adventure. Unfortunately, his mother and father, the dominant class, owners of the means of production, have reduced him to the miserable conditions of a slave and thus oblige him to eat what he doesn't want to eat, do stupid, meaningless homework—can there be any greater alienation?—and go to bed when there are still so many entertaining things to do. Adults are guilty of his unhappiness. But the day will come when the shout of revolution arises: "Children of the whole world! Unite!" Children will take over. The dominant adults will not be shot, as they well deserve, because children know how to forgive. It will be a classless society, the return to Paradise. When this moment arrives, Calvin will be an extraordinary revolutionary leader.

And then, out of the blue, the moment will come, gloriously announced by the hair cropping up in places previously smooth. Ah! The hair! Finally. How much envy and how much fantasy were teased up in the heads of boys and girls as they thought about those symbols of the condition of adulthood.

The psychological importance of that hair has not yet been sufficiently analyzed. My clinical research on the subject led me to a curious discovery: the hair is responsible for a syndrome characteristic of adolescence, yet to be described in scientific compendiums. I have baptized it with the term "the Samson Syndrome."

As you know from biblical mythology, Samson was a hero of uncommon strength. He, alone, defeated an entire army, an army armed with swords and lances, he himself armed with no more than the jawbone of an ass. Next to Samson, Rambo was anemic. Well Samson's strength was in his hair. All Delilah had to do was give the hero a haircut for his strength to wither like a punctured balloon.

The Samson Syndrome is a mental disturbance that causes adolescents to identify the growth of their hair with the growth of their strength. And this illusion is confirmed in their heads by the development and growth of organs adjacent to the hair, newly sprouted, which start working at a touch of the "start button," even under the most adverse conditions, such as early winter mornings. Which contrast with the paternal Studebakers that, under similar conditions, demand a new battery and only work after several attempts, their operation interrupted by coughs, breathlessness, and sudden shutdown, to the embarrassment of all.

Yes, the children are no longer children. Besides the growth of the hair, there is the growth of the body. Now the children looking up in the elevator have become enormous adolescents who look down. They are bigger than their parents. Not only bigger but better. The latest model. The model of the parents is already obsolete. "The elderly." Already out of production. Old Studebakers, rambling along, dented, smoke spewing from the tailpipe. To go out with them is an embarrassment.

The glorious moment: the taking of power. The revolution. Adolescence has arrived. To understand adolescents, you need to understand the sociology and psychology of revolutionaries.

The oppressed class does not go around with the dominant class. It doesn't go to the same places. It doesn't speak the same language. It doesn't want to converse. The worker does not converse with the boss. Workers demand their rights. If they don't get them, they go on strike. Teens don't want to chat with mom and dad. They no longer visit the family farm. They don't spend New Year's Eve at home. They don't listen to the same music. If it's prohibited, it has to be transgressed. With the teen, a new order is begun. The teen is a militant. Adolescence is an anarchic revolutionary party. If the political situation were anything else, your kid's place would be at demonstrations, possibly as a guerrilla. But today, the way things are, the teen can't pass up a party.

The Crowd

A dash of madness increases the pleasure of life. Such is the case of cinema. You go there, sit down, and watch the play of colored lights projected on a screen. You know it's all a lie. Nonetheless, you tremble in fear, your heart beats fast, your blood pressure goes up, you sweat with trepidation, you laugh, you cry. It's an event of insanity. You are taking in images as if they were reality. But if you didn't give yourself over to two hours of this insanity, watching a movie would be as thrilling as reading a phone book. After two hours, the lights come up, you leave the insanity and walk firmly back into reality.

The difference between your insanity and that of the insane is that the insane never leave the cinema. The movie never ends. The lights never come back on. The insane never think that what is going through their heads is just a film. They think it's real.

The one who is not insane is the one who doesn't trust her thoughts. She knows her head is tricky—a movie show. Nothing guarantees that her thoughts—that which seems to be projected on the screen of her consciousness—are true. Reason is distrusted. When a person says, "I am sure!" she is confessing: "I have no doubts about my thoughts!" Consequently, she is in a psychotic event.

Adolescence is the age of certainty. Adolescents don't distrust their ideas and opinions. They piously believe what their thoughts tell them. So the logical conclusion is that ideas different from their own can only be wrong. This explains their difficulty in dealing with contrary opinion. "I know what I am doing" is the standard answer they use to disregard warnings about a problematic course of action.

Certainty of thought is always accompanied by a sense of omnipotence. The gods know everything and are invulnerable. So they have no fear of doing risky things—drag races, Russian roulette, a game of chicken—because nothing can happen to them. Serious accidents only happen to others. "I can smoke weed and sniff cocaine without fear. I know what I'm doing. I'll never get addicted. Only the weak get addicted. But I'm strong."

That's why programs that seek to warn teens about the dangers of drugs are doomed to fail. They are developed under the presupposition that if teens recognize dangers, they will avoid them. But that is the same as trying to dissuade the mountain climber from her dream of scaling the Himalayas because it's dangerous, or to convince Amyr Klink to cancel his trip to the South Pole because of the danger of the seas. Mountain climbers and ocean explorers go on their adventures precisely to defy danger. It's the danger that creates emotion.

That's how adolescents are. They want risk. Contrary to the mountain climber and sailor, however, they believe that nothing can happen to them. They don't go down the road of drugs in ignorance of the danger. They do it to defy the danger, evidently in the certainty that nothing will happen to him. This psychotic illusion has an aggravating factor: the reinforcement of the "crowd."

Sociology gave the name "relevant others" to people whom I consider when acting. These others are an "audience" before whom I represent my role and whose applause I seek and whose boos I fear. Parents are children's most important "significant others." At any given moment, children are seeking their parents' looks of approval. Adolescence is the moment when the parents are replaced by the "crowd."

The crowd is tyrannical. It imposes and demands. Adolescents must obey. It was 10:30 p.m. The mother went to her 13-year-old daughter's bedroom for a loving good-night kiss on the sleeping innocent's cheek. What she found was a note on the empty bed. "I can't let my friends down. I went to the party."

The crowd creates a lovely feeling of fraternity. Everyone is confirmed. Everyone does the same things together. Everyone is a "conspirator." But as they do that, the crowd extracts a sense of identity from isolated individuals. Without the crowd, the teen is just a face with no mirror. In the crowd, shy and respectable individuals independently turn into immoral savages. It's "crowds" that lynch. Individually, we are moral beings. In the crowd, personal responsibility disappears. The crowd is the law. It imposes. The crowd decides about clothes, sneakers, nightclubs, music, weed, coke, hook-ups. Woe unto the one who disobeys.

In relation to adult society, the adolescent is a revolutionary. She's ready to transgress against everything to create a new order. In relation to her "crowd," she's a reluctant sheep without her own ideas and submissive to the authority of the group. Adolescence is a perpetual game of Simon Says.

Remember what I wrote in another chronicle, that there are two types of adolescent: the mature and the gullible. Everything I have just said applies to the second group.

Nothing can be done about this. Fortunately, angels of all kinds arrive from the heavens. I suggest that parents beseech angels specializing in watching over teens to take care of their sons and daughters. And that, for their own good, they invoke the angels of sleep and dreams. If nothing can be done, at least their sleep should be calm, their dreams soft.

To the (Possible) Thrushes

Somebody I don't know, after seeing the smoke I blew regarding adolescents, concluded that I must have something against them. "Rubem doesn't like teenagers."

There's a pinch of truth in that. And parents would agree with me: if they lose sleep over their sons and daughters, it's because there's something in their teens that they don't like. If they liked it, they'd sleep well and not look for therapists to help. Life is more complex than liking or not liking—*that is not the question*. The question is liking and not liking at the same time. That's what makes them suffer.

I imagined that this person I don't know, if she saw Michelangelo furiously attacking a block of marble with a hammer and chisel, would ask, "Really, what does Michelangelo have against marble?"

Yes, he has a lot against the block of marble. Because the *Pietà* is stored inside it. You have to not feel sorry for the marble because the *Pietà* comes out of its tomb. Love, for the *Pietà*, has no pity... Where would the *Pietà* be if Michelangelo had been complacent about the block of marble?

Education is an art. And there is nothing more contrary to art than to leave the raw material as it is. The only people who do this are those who don't dream. But, disgracefully, feelings of parental guilt turn into complacency, and their hammers and chisels turn into gelatin. The stone continues to be stone. You have to understand that love is tough.

I recall a paragraph from Nietzsche:

> My burning desire to create continuously pushes me in the direction of man. That's how the hammer is also pushed in the direction of stone. Oh, mankind! An image sleeps in the stone, the image of my images. Yes, it sleeps inside the hardest and ugliest stone... Now my hammer fights furiously against its prison. Chunks of rock rain from the stone...

Ridendo dicere severun: Laughing, talk of serious things. Laughter is my hammer and chisel. I don't know if you have noticed that, in all that I write on adolescents, someone got left out. Included were parents and their afflictions: I wrote for them. Adolescents and their crowds were included: I wrote in the hope that the parents should show them my mirror and they would see themselves as parrots and carriers of the Samson Syndrome. I wished that once they had looked at themselves through my eyes, they would see how they are funny and entertaining. It isn't possible to think about their craziness without a good laugh. And that this makes them laugh at themselves. At the moment we laugh at ourselves, the spell is broken.

Who got left out? The lone teen—that one who has no crowd, whose telephone remains silent, who on Saturday night stays home listening to music in his or her room.

When I go out for an early morning walk, groups of teens pass me on their way to school. I can spot the groups, which go happily along parroting their things in the light joy of belonging to a crowd. They talk about kisses, sex, and parties.

These don't touch my emotions. The ones that touch me are the ones who are always alone. They are different. In clothes, body, and mannerism, their eyes fixed on the ground. They have no stories of kisses or parties. I am touched by them because I was like that. I was alone in my adolescence. I was a kid from a small town in the interior of Minas Gerais before my family moved to Rio de Janeiro. And my father committed a big mistake inspired by his sincere desire to give me the best. He enrolled me in one of the city's high schools for the elite, the famous Colégio Andrews.

Albert Camus said he had always been happy until he entered the Lyceum. In the Lyceum he began to make comparisons. I could say the same thing. I learned the motives behind other people's laughter. I spoke slowly and lyrically, uttering the typical *"Uai"* exclamation typical of Minas Gerais, rolling hard R's in words like *carne* and *mar* in a hillbilly accent, twisting my tongue around the hard sound. The way I dressed was hillbilly, too. And the cash I carried was the cash of poor people. And the country clubs they went to weren't mine. I didn't go to any country club whatsoever. Naturally I was never invited to parties. And if I had been, I wouldn't have gone. Nor did I ever invite a schoolmate to my house. I was afraid my house was too poor.

And that's what I would like to tell lonely adolescents today, teens with no crowd, no parties, no stories of kisses and love affairs to talk about, the Saturday nights at home, the silent telephone: you are my companions. I walked the same roads as you.

But I am grateful to life for having been that way. Because it was through suffering this terrible solitude that I went about producing my pearls. "Happy oysters make no pearls." So I started walking alone down roads where the other teens didn't go: music, the mystic, art, literature, poetry, philosophy. All those solitary worlds you can go to only if alone. Going down those roads I discovered those who seemed like me. Zarathustra, for example, who saw himself as a tree growing at the edge of a cliff, his long branches reaching over the abyss. I wanted to be like that, too.

And that's how I started to see parrots with a certain sense of superiority. Of course psychoanalysts, big on interpretation, would hurry to inform me that this was no more than a compensation for my sentiments of inferiority. In other words, sinister Kleinians. The fact is, compensation or not, the joy I found in my work has been greater than the sadness of my condition as a solitary adolescent. For me, the solitude went on to become a source of happiness. I didn't need to scream like a parrot to be heard.

Parrots scream, and everyone hears it, even if they don't want to. But the song of the solitary thrush at the end of day somewhere in the forest makes everyone hush up and listen. This is what I want to tell you solitary teens: there is much beauty hidden in your sadness. Don't feel sorry for yourselves. Get to work with your hammer and chisel.

III

Maturity

Soufflé Time

Our subject today is cooking. I have chosen the gastronomic topic soufflé.

Soufflés can be made with practically anything. There are soufflés of asparagus, cheese, chayote, shrimp, banana, chocolate, salmon, strawberry, ham, carrot, and so on. This variety of soufflés owes itself to the fact that the ingredient which characterizes a soufflé isn't the thing it's made of but the ethereal, pneumatic substance that goes into all of them.

I found it strange, then, that this substance, the soul of the soufflé, never gets mentioned in the cookbooks that I look through. I went to the famous *New York Times Cookbook* to see if it said something about the soul of soufflés. I read the recipe for "cheese soufflé." The necessary ingredients are listed: butter, flour, milk, salt, Worcestershire sauce, Jamaica peppers, shredded cheese, eggs. That's all. But the soul of the soufflé, without which it cannot be made, isn't mentioned. Dona Benta's book is no better. See the recipe for "cod soufflé": cod, potatoes, milk, eggs, parmesan cheese, butter, seedless raisins, and olives. Again, total silence on the soul of the soufflé.

The word soufflé, for those who don't know, comes from the French. Soufflé comes from the word *souffler,* "to blow." The soul of the soufflé is the air. That's where the soufflé gets its pneumatic and spiritual qualities. The soul of s*ouffler* is wind and spirit. If it weren't for the snobbish craze of finding the French word more elegant, if the soufflé had been invented in Minas Gerais, for sure the word for it would be *assoprado,* or "blown." Chayote blown, shrimp blown, asparagus blown, etc. Which should not be shocking in that, according to what it says in the cookbook *Fogão de Lenha* [wood-fired cook stove], which records some 300 years of cooking in Minas Gerais, there was some kind of sweet called "Little Blown Girls, which was made of beaten egg whites, three pounds of sugar, an ounce of bitters, a little carmine. If the housewife can make Little Blown Girls, she can make blowns, too.

If you aren't convinced, remember that the essential element in the making of a soufflé is the whites of the eggs, beaten until stiff. But what is the purpose of these egg whites? It's obvious and simple: the whites are nets for catching air. The circular-rotational whipping motion of the fork beating the whites is the same as the motion of a fisherman throwing his net to catch fish. But here, what you want to catch is the air, which egg whites do so well that they go from the consistency of goo to that of foam: thousands of little transparent bubbles, each one of them with a tiny bit of air stuck inside.

From this pneumatic and spiritual quality of the soufflé comes its essential characteristic: the soufflé is fffffluffffy. You can't say fffff-fluffffy without blowing air through your lips. Webster's dictionary defines soufflé as a *fluffy* baked dish.

This pneumatic characteristic of the soufflé, its glory, is, unfortunately, also its weakness. Because everything that is full of air, such as balls and balloons, turns mushy and empty at the most minute puncture. The same thing happens to the poor soufflé. It has to be eaten as soon as it comes out of the oven because its erection is precarious. If it cools down or gets hit by a puff of cold air, it suffers a seizure: first, a slight tremor, then vertical and horizontal movements—6.5 on the Richter scale—and then there's a cry for help as the golden-brown blush on the surface suddenly sinks to the bottom of the form.

I remember when this happened once in my house. I was a boy. We had guests for dinner. Astolfina, our cook, prepared a wonderful soufflé. But it got hit by a waft of cold air and turned mushy. Astolfina was desperate. She decided it would be worth heroic measures. She went into the back yard and cut a hollow papaya twig and carefully threaded it into the soufflé, the same way one inserts the pin of an air pump into a ball. And she blew softly. The soufflé seemed to resuscitate, filling up again, becoming as beautiful as it had been. But as soon as she extracted the twig, the soufflé fell back down. There is no way to fix a sunken soufflé.

As a patient of mine once said, thinking about the fate of women, "It's like a soufflé. Doctors say that menopause is climacteric. I say menopause is soufflé time. Until then, the flesh behaved itself with relative elegance. The power of air gave it lightness and held it up. But all of a sudden, the forces of the Earth become stronger, and everything that floated in the air begins to weigh down. And it falls. I don't need to name the parts that fall nor describe their flaccid and mushy condition.

I had to bow before that powerful metaphor. But I thought to myself, "What about men? Is there a soufflé time for them, too?"

Soufflé time is the time for generalized panic, like Astolfina's, everyone trying to use a papaya twig to raise up what has fallen. Diets, seaweed creams, turtle soap, hair dye, skin cleansing, gyms, plastic surgery, girdles, acupuncture, prosthetics...

All futile. There is no way to refill a sunken soufflé. The little straw always fails. All you can do is laugh when it falls. And it's good to know that the fallen soufflé, even though it isn't as beautiful as the risen, is quite delicious if served with spices and humor and a good laugh.

On Male Sexuality (1)

It's becoming an embarrassing routine. I agree to speak on a subject, and as soon as I sit down to put my ideas on paper, I discover that I don't know anything about it. This happened once, and now it has happened again. I agreed to speak about male sexuality. But when I put myself to thinking, I came to the unheard-of conclusion that male sexuality does not exist. Which doesn't mean it wasn't a fascinating challenge, quite like that of theologians who, in the same way, talk about nonexistent objects.

I started far from anything to do with bed. Rather, I spoke about things to do with the table. Table and bed, seemingly so different in appearance, have something in common: they are places to eat. The verb "eat" is used indifferently to indicate pleasures of the mouth and pleasures of sex. Tita, from the film *Like Water to Chocolate*, whom I imagine was inspired by the Gospel, developed a means of making love through cooking. Such are the Evangelicals who say that eating is a sacrament: to eat food is to eat who served it. "Take it, eat it, this is my body." And so it was that I tried to enter the mysteries of sexuality through the mysteries of food.

I went to a medical book, seeking enlightenment into the universal science of eating. There I found a description of the apparatus and functions of digestion. A transversal cut across the human body showed the mouth, the esophagus, the stomach, the intestines, the anus. In all this, human beings are alike: food enter at one extreme and leaves by the other. This is true of Hottentot Pygmies, Eskimos, Bruna Lombardi,[4] the pope, the queen of England. For the apparatus and function of digestion, a universal science does, in fact, exist.

I looked for information about foods—for it would be expected that where there's talk of digestion, there's also talk of what's eaten. It was futile. I had to go to a bookstore. And there I lingered with wonderful modern books on cooking: Chinese, Japanese, Italian, French, Arabic, Greek, Russian, Spanish, from Minas Gerais, from Bahia: all different. Infinite are the ways of eating; infinite are ways of pleasure through the mouth; such various types of spice, such various types of ingredients, the aromas, the colors, the manners, the etiquettes. In one place, the epitome of refinement is to burp loudly and to make noise while eating with an open mouth. In others, that's prohibited. People eat at tables, they eat on the floor, with fork, knife and spoon, with little sticks, with the hand. There's no right way. Everything de-

---

[4] Brazilian actress renowned for, among other things, her beauty.

pends on place. That's why there can't be a universal science of the act of eating. There is only the art, which varies.

I returned to the medical book and looked for information about the sex organs. Just as with the organs of digestion, I again found the images—everything the same for the whole world: the Hottentots, the Eskimos, Bruna Lombardi, the pope, the queen of England. They all worked the same way. On the apparatus and reproductive functions, there can be a universal science.

I looked for information about the ways of eating in bed—for it would be expected where there's talk about the sex organs, there's also talk of sexuality. It was futile. So I went to literature, the experience and imagination that would come to my aid. And it told me that eating at the table and eating in bed are the same thing. There is no science of either. There isn't ONE feminine sexuality, just as there isn't ONE male sexuality. With one clarinet you can play anything from a sad adagio to a Brazilian *chorinho*.[5] It all depends on the taste and ability of the player. Just as there are infinite ways to play the clarinet, there are infinite ways to eat in bed.

It came into my head, without my having to do any scientific research (scientists always need research to conclude: they think slowly...), that the term male sexuality refers to a vast, expandable fan of variations: the *Kama Sutra*, that menu of the bed, is extremely diverse, including foods and means of eating for all tastes—the widest variety of

---

[5] A lively Brazilian genre often featuring a clarinet.

ingredients and spices. It all depends on the taste and the ability of the one who's going to chow down...

At one extreme of the fan of masculine sexuality is the sexuality inspired in the ways that pigs eat: corn cobs, yams, leftover beans and strawberry tarts are all devoured in one mouthful, the taste of it not mattering, everything at the same time, without discrimination. The only thing that matters is the "finally."

At the other extreme is the sexuality inspired by cooking inspired by Babette.[6] Everything is delicate, subtle, and inebriating, even the napkins and the position of the candles. Everything is thought of as a work of art. But, as you know, this is something for special days, festive days...

Right in the middle of the fan is daily sexuality, the trivial of the quotidian: the rice and beans, the meat and collards, the lettuce and tomato, the homemade food that can be served reheated in a mixture with hot pepper. Which reminds me of a love story. The wife—she loved her husband so much!—made grits every day, a heavy food for keeping one's strength up. It went on like that forever with heart-touching fidelity, without fail. Every morning, there it was before her husband, a plate of grits that he ate right up. Until the unexpected occurred. She got old, got sick, couldn't get out of bed. What would become of her poor husband without his grits? Devastated, she called him to explain that, sadly, on that day, she couldn't make his grits. His

---

[6] Protagonist of the Danish film Babette's Feast and a short story of the same title by Karen Blixen.

face broke into a wide smile. "Don't worry, my dear. To tell you the truth, I don't even like grits…"

On Male Sexuality (II)

The ferocious North American feminists say that the idea of a father God, masculine, is an invention of men, with the purpose of making women submissive to the phallus. For that reason they are trying to change the sex of God. For them, God isn't a god; she's a goddess.

I'll sign that petition. I think they have total reason. The divine powers that decide the fates of men must be feminine. If the divine powers were masculine, they would not allow the evils that are done to men. All one has to do is assess the asymmetry between men and women to see that humble situation of the men.

Men, fooled by the fantasy that they have something that women lack, don't take into account their own fragility. And, in an incomprehensible blindness to anatomic and physiological facts, they say that they "eat" women.[7] Pure error. To eat is an act in which something is put into the mouth, the mouth being an empty orifice that extracts from the referred-to object, through rhythmic movements, its sub-

---

[7] In the Brazilian vernacular, to "eat" (*comer*) a woman means to have sex with her.

stance and juices. Now, the anatomy is clear: it's the woman who is the empty orifice that receives the male object, which in the end appears mushy and drained. Woman is mouth: man is fruit. In the end, the only thing left is the peel of the orange. At the end of every sexual act, the man loses his penis. The woman, on the other hand, eats and grows fat. Psychoanalysis customarily says that women suffer from a "castration complex" because something is missing. Totally wrong. The ones who suffer this pain are the men. They are the ones who lose the penis at the end of the sexual act. With what they don't have, women can have as many of what the men have as they want. In the words of Norman O. Brown, what happens with the penis is a crowning followed by decapitation.

The second asymmetry is another punishment from the goddesses. On a par with anatomo-functional asymmetry, the goddess imposes on man a punishment of honesty. He can't hide it or pretend. He can't, by rational decision, give his penis an order. The penis has its own ideas. It doesn't obey. It just does what it pleases.

It's different for women. She doesn't run the risk of humiliation. By means of a rational decision, she can have a relationship with the person she loves. She can pretend, and the other will never know. Maybe the greatest pleasure in a sexual relationship is the pleasure of being the object of someone else's pleasure. "Someone desires me. I can satisfy that desire." Babette, marvelous cook, took no pleasure in eating the food that she prepared. She only tasted it. Her pleasure was in giving pleasure. This is as valid for eating at the table as for eating in bed. And the woman is like Babette. She can give pleasure whenever she wishes. That can't happen with a man.

The venerable St. Augustine said, in his *De Civitate Dei*, that this was the primary punishment that divinities inflicted on man: they separated the penis from reason so that at inappropriate moments, the former would set itself to doing things it shouldn't, and at appropriate moments to not do what it should. That's why the gods, feeling sorry for men, covered them with clothes: to hide their shame. And is there anything more shameful than a penis numb to the desire of a woman? Zorba said that that was the only sin for which man would go to Hell. St. Augustine concluded that the ideal would be for the male organ to function the same way the finger functions, moving without ever disobeying, as ordered by reason. To which every man ever born or to be born says, "Amen!"

Then comes the fantasy of "she's just too much sand for my little truck." Of course there's always the recourse of making two trips. But the asymmetry continues. In culinary terms, "my food is too little for her hunger." In technical terms: "I, as an object of desire, am too small for her desire." And women are the first to speak out on the enormous size of their desire. Adélia Prado said, "For my desire, the sea is but a drop." Oh! So then men need to be gods to satisfy this oceanic desire!

So men start to fear women's desire. "Better a woman with no desire. For if she has no desire, I won't go through the humiliation of not being able to satisfy it." For that reason men of generations past want virgin brides, not for reasons of religious purity, but to prevent the possibility of comparison. Men can't stand imagining that the desire of their beloved, which he can't satisfy, could be satisfied by someone else. Hence the terror of a woman's infidelity. No, don't be fooled. The wound isn't from being without her; the pain isn't the loss of her. The greater pain, intolerable, is narcissism. For "to be unfaithful to me and abandon me, she is proclaiming to the four winds my incapacity to satisfy her desire: she reveals the secret of my incompetence." What is intolerable to the man isn't the absence of his woman but the looks of his peers—other men. Sexual identity is also defined "homosexually" through its confirmation by others of the same sex. "My masculinity should be recognized not only by the woman but also by my peers." Saunas are still sanctuaries of recognition. But if the woman doesn't have desire, the man will be protected from this horrible metaphysical danger. Virginity, the excision of the clitoris practiced by some African tribes, sexual indifference, and, at its most extreme, crimes of passion, are means of possessing a woman through the destruction of her desire. "A woman without desire is always mine."

The brute appearance, the muscles sculpted by weightlifting, the tales of sexual prowess, the visual productions in accordance with male standards—all of these are tricks of a fearful being faced with the fascinating mystery of women. "So weak, so fragile—and still, it is before her that I will be exposed. It will be she who exposes whether I am the food that can end her hunger." Those who do not feel anxiety are those who don't understand, like dogs: they still haven't heard the news. Soon her flesh will surprise them with the message. And from then on, they will be permanently lost.

Now tell me: do the goddesses need to do such evil to men?

For a Son

I've said before that I think the custom of blowing out birthday candles is morbid. A candle should never be blown out. There's always the danger that the gods won't understand what we're asking for when we extinguish the flame, a symbol of life. To avoid misunderstandings, I prefer to do the opposite: to light a candle. The gods will understand what I'm asking for. And that's what I do on my birthday, my son: I light a candle...

A candle is a magical thing. Its flame illuminates dark corners in the caverns of memory. In its light appear paintings, photos, images that an Unknown, down through the years, has hung on its walls. St. Augustine thought the same way. In his *Confessions*, he, too, describes memory as a deep cavern, so deep that certain images, to be remembered, have to be unearthed.

In *A História sem Fim (The Story without End)*, the boy Bastian Baltazar Bux is lost in Fantasy. He needs to drink from the Fountain of the Waters of Life to be able to go back home. But to find the path, he has to remember something that he no longer remembers: an image of love. In search of this lost memory, he arrives at the Mine of Images.

"Who are you?" Bastian asks the guard of the mine.

"I am Yor, the one called the Blind Miner. But I am blind only where there is light. In my mine, where total darkness reigns, I can see."

Across the immense, silent, frozen plain Bastian saw images on the snow, as if they were precious jewels encrusted in white silk. They were thin chips of a kind of transparent and colored mica of all sizes...

"They are the world's forgotten dreams," Yor explained.

He continued: "You seek the Waters of Life. You wanted to be capable of love, to be able to return to your world. To love—it's easy to say. But the Waters of Life are going to ask: Whom? One does not love in general. If you are not capable of answering, you may not drink. Therefore, only a forgotten dream that you find here will be able to help you..."

For days and weeks Bastian walked among the images stuck in the snow in search of his dream. Futilely. All the images left him indifferent. Then Yor said to him, "You need to go down into the deepest part of the mine and dig..."

For days and days Bastian worked, stuck in the center of the earth like a child in the womb of a mother, searching for his forgotten dream. Until one day, a new image... It was a new feeling, coming from afar like a wave in the sea rising up, turning into a wall of water as high as a house and dragging everything with it. His heart ached. It felt as if it weren't big enough for such longing...

One remembers many things with neither pain nor longing. They are the commonplace things that live on the surface of the earth, within eyesight, within reach of the hands, within reach of words... In the caverns of memories, however, the only images stored are the ones that hurt to be remembered. They are the images of longing. Images of longing are pieces of our own body that time has taken. Everything that is loved is transformed into part of the person, the same way that Ricardo Reis said:

That bush
withers, and with it goes
part of my life.
In everything I've seen, I am a part...

Well that's how it was, my son, seeing time passing you along. I invoked the gods and lit my candle to look in the memory caverns for the images of longing that I would like to keep repeating forever.

The first was that of a six-year-old boy walking alone in a desert in a faraway country with a strange language. You had to learn the path. My desire, as a father, was to go on holding your hand, to always be nearby so that the little boy would not be afraid. But the time had come when the little boy had to go out alone into that unknown world. And there I remained at the window, watching you walking on that cold autumn morning. And suddenly I understood that that scene was going to repeat many more times. And I would have to remain watching from afar, from the window, while you walked on alone.

The second picture I found strange. It was all black, with no light at all. I looked but could not see anything. I realized that it was night. A bedroom. We had just returned from a foreign country. It was in the sinister years of the military repression in Brazil. I rolled around in bed, unable to sleep, thinking the thoughts one thinks when fear is mixed with air. My only company was the snoring of those who were asleep. I felt absolutely alone with my anguish. At least that's what I thought. But all of a sudden, I heard the voice of a child:

"Daddy!"

"What is it, my son?"

"I like you a lot."

For me, at that moment, the dictatorship ended, in the middle of my laughter and my crying.

The last picture is of a day many years later. It was the end of an afternoon. I went for a ride in the car to watch the sunset. I was driving along on the outskirts of Castelo when I saw, far away, up ahead, a young man on a motorcycle. Motorcycles always scare me, but that scene was nice. It was as if he were riding a wild horse. I could not make out his face. Against the backdrop of the setting sun, his hair was in flames. His profile was golden, like a Nordic hero. The motorcycle moved slowly. There was no rush. I came closer to have a look and pass around. It was you...and I began to laugh.

I think I will know how to answer when the Waters of Life ask me, "Who?"

Happy birthday.

IV

Old Age

Old Age

And all of a sudden, my eyes opened. I saw that I was old. No, it wasn't the sum of years lived that led me to that conclusion. Actually, there is an old age that's an entity of the exterior world that can be measured by calendars, clocks, and the decadence of the body: geriatrics. But there is another...

I laughed to read an item in the newspaper: "Elderly man of 50 run over." I imagined that the man of 50 had been run over twice: by the car and by the news. And the news most certainly caused greater damage.

Something like that happened with me. It was a young woman who looked at me with a sweet smile and suspended me in ephemeral romantic parentheses in a subway car and then, with a clear gesture, offered me her seat. The kind gesture had the effect of getting run over. She had silently said, "I like you. You look like the father I'd like to have had." The romantic parentheses popped like a soap bubble.

I remember that, as I took the seat—as her terrible gesture of love obliged me to do—some lines from Eliot came to me:

(They will say: "How his hair is growing thin!")
My morning coat, my collar mounting firmly to the chin,
My necktie rich and modest, but asserted by a simple pin
(They will say: "But how his arms and legs are thin!")

For some years I thought that it had been at that moment that the revelation had occurred. But I changed my mind. Riobaldo[8] showed me that old age isn't that which occurs when the marks of time wrinkle the surface of the body. Old age is something that goes on happening inside, not unlike the way a flower grows in a garden. What he taught me was: "All longing is a kind of old age."

His sentence was in such perfect harmony with my feelings that I needed no further proof. He gave a name to that which I felt without knowing how to say it. Old age is missing something.

That explains why there are young people, children even, who have lived but a handful of years yet are already old. It's that longing can blossom even early in life. That was the case of the boy Miguilim, who, according to the narrator, every day "took a little swallow of old age," with the explanation that, for him, "the days didn't fit within time. Everything was late." (João Guimarães Rosa, *Manuelzão e Miguilim*, pp. 77 and 60.)

---

[8] Riobaldo is the protagonist of Guimarães Rosa's modernist classic, *Grande Sertão: Veredas*. He spoke wise words in the mysterious vernacular of Brazil's northeast.

Eliot was not a boy. He was already 32. But no one is old at 32. Meanwhile, however, he wrote: "Here I am, an old man in a dry month..." (T.S. Eliot, *The Complete Poems and Plays*, p. 21.)

So I noticed that old age isn't something new. It had always lived within me. Ever since I was a boy, I seemed like Miguilim. Like Miguilim, I took a little swallow of old age every day. And even my early days were late. I was always missing something, longing for something without knowing what it was. Missing something without knowing what can seem senseless since missing something is always a longing for something: a face, a place, a time past. But poets know that this is not the case. Álvaro de Campos spoke of "a prognostic and empty longing," and he said that "the memory of something that you don't remember chills the soul." (Álvoro de Campos, *Poemas*, pp. 118 and 29.) And Adélia Prado, in that joking and jovial tone she uses to hide pain, wrote, "Ah, longing! My God, of what? I no longer know." (Adélia Prado, *Poesia Reunida*, p. 63.)

Have you never felt that? An inexplicable longing for something but you don't know what it is? Longing, then, is like a sadness in your very being, without an object. When you feel that, don't get distressed. It's that your eyes are moving through a mysterious forest where poetry is born. They are the forests of longing. All poets are like Miguilim: they were born old. Carlos Drummond de Andrade wrote this lovely poem (Oh, that little word, "lovely." What does it intend to say? It intends to say that the thing which we call "lovely" makes love without our soul. When we say that something is lovely, therefore, we are confessing how we are inside...) As I was saying, Drummond wrote this lovely poem titled *Ausência* (*Absence*):

For a long time I believed that absence is a lacking.
And, ignorant, I rued the lack.
Today I do not rue it.
There is no lacking in absence.
Absence is a being in me.
And I feel it, white, so clinging, cuddled in my arms,
so I laugh and dance and think of joyous exclamations,
because absence, this assimilated absence,
no one can any longer steal from me.

To miss something is to feel absence: you feel longing because the beloved thing is absent. So I think that Drummond wouldn't mind if, where "absence" is written, we read "longing." But, since longing is old age, the poem *Ausência* can be read as a poem of *Old Age*. Swap the words and reread the poem. You will see yourself, as Drummond did, laughing and dancing and thinking up joyous exclamations and repeating:

Why does no one take this old age,
this assimilated old age, away from me...

Miguilim's Eyes

Something has changed in my eyes. I suspected illness, so I went to look it up in the texts of ophthalmology. But no matter how much I looked, I couldn't find anything at all, be it in chapter titles, be it in the index. Doctors told me I was looking in the wrong books. They said that it would be better if I had read books of poetry. "Longing," they explained, isn't an illness of the eyes. There are no eye drops, no glasses, no surgery that cures it. I accept the verdict of science, but I still don't understand.

Please, if you can, explain this strange transformation in my eyes. It must be a rare disease, some unknown syndrome as yet undescribed but worth discussion at a congress. The transformation is this: when longing hits me, my eyes stop seeing what they used to see right in front of them and start seeing things they didn't used to see. In a Chico Buarque song, a mother looked at the bedroom of her dead son and flowers in a vase: certainly an insanity of longing. She saw something that others did not see. It's like what happens when you look at the colorful layouts of the book *Olho Mágico* (*Magic Eye*) with a blank stare. What the authors are presenting as a novelty is something I've known for a while. First the colors change. After you don't see them, they appear. And everything becomes different.

The one who told me to read poetry was right. I remembered that in fact I had already read about this transformation of sight in a text by Octavio Paz.

> Every day we cross the same street or the same garden. Every afternoon our eyes pass by the same reddened wall made of bricks and urban time.
>
> All of a sudden, on just any old day, the road leads to another wall, the garden has just blossomed, the tired wall is covered with signs of something. We've never seen them before, and now we're shocked by the way they are: so many and so overwhelmingly real.
>
> What we're seeing for the first time we have already seen before. The wall, the street, the garden were all somewhere where we've never been. And the surprise is followed by nostalgia. It seems that we remember and want to go back there to that place where things are always like that, bathed in ancient light and at the same time just now blossoming. We, too, are from there. A gust of wind hits us in the forehead. We are enchanted, suspended in the middle of an immobile afternoon.

That's how my eyes get, and that's how my world gets when longing snuggles into my lap, when old age plays with me. My normal eyes see the streets, the walls, the gardens, just as they are, the same way they would appear if we took a photograph of them. But, charmed by longing, my eyes become endowed with strange, magic powers. They see the absences, that which isn't there but which the heart desires.

When I was in elementary school, they made me memorize a lot of things. I've forgotten most of them. Some I learned by heart. Those I still remember. I distinguish between "memorize" and "learn by heart." Memorizing is mechanical. Learning by heart, as the words reveal, is a matter of love. To learn by heart is to write on the heart. What is written on my heart becomes part of my body. It is never forgotten. Adélia's words: "That which the memory loved remains eternal."

My meditation on eyes and longing brings me to the memory of this poem by Tomás Antônio Gonzaga, learned by heart. If I learned it as a boy, it's because it comes mixed with a swallow of old age that I drank every day.

Perchance are these
the gentle places,
where I spent the luscious years?
Are these the meadows,
where I played,
while grazed the tame herd
that Alceu left me?

From that cliff
a river fell;
to the sound of the sigh
I sometimes slept!
Now snowy foam,
covers the broken rock no more:
It seems the river
has turned the course back.

My verses, joyous,
here repeat;
the words echo
three times spoke.
If I call for him,
he will not answer;
he seems to be hidden,
tired of giving me
the sighs that I gave him.

Here a stream
flowed serenely
along banks covered
with flowers and hay;
to the left arises
a dense wood,
and the rushed time,

which respects nothing,
now everything's changed.

But how to discuss it?
Perchance might
all have changed
in the space of a day?
There are springs,
and leafy ash;
meadows proffer flowers,
and the waterfall
which has never dried up,
now runs.

My soul, which had
freed my will,
now feels
love and longing.
The gentle places,
that have pleased me so,
Ah! they have not changed;
my eyes have changed,
so sad am I.

                                    Are these the places?
                                        These are; but I
                                  the same am not, no.

Marília, you call?
Wait, that I may go.

And, to bring it to an end, one more swallow of old age, a verse from Rilke: "Who has turned us round like this, so that, whatever we do, we always look like someone departing? Just as they will turn, stop, linger, for one last time, on that last hill, that displays their whole valley—so we live and are always leaving."

Old age is like that. Miguilim knows this quite well.

The Useless Tree

This story is attributed to Chuang-Tzu, the third of the great masters of Taoism:

Nan-Po Tzu-ki crossed Chang's hill. He noticed a surprisingly large tree. It's shade could cover a thousand four-horse coaches.

"What tree is this?" Tzu-ki asked. "What is it good for?" Looking at it from below, he saw that its small, curved and crooked branches couldn't be turned into beams or rafters. Looking at it from above, he saw that its great trunk, knotty and cracked, couldn't be used to build anything whatsoever, not even coffins. Anyone who licked its leaves would end up with an ulcerated tongue covered with abscesses. Just smelling the tree made a person dizzy and inebriated for three days.

Tzu-ki concluded:

"This tree really is of no use. That's why it has managed to reach such a size. Ah, divine man, you are no more than wood that cannot be used."

I recalled this solitary and extraordinary tree on Chang's hill when I read the news of a man as solitary and even more extraordinary than the tree... It could only be the divine man Chuang-Tzu was referring to. His name: Takeshi Nojima. A Japanese immigrant [to Brazil], 80 years old, he'd sold tomatoes, raised silkworms, and owned a grocery. He was studying for the entrance exam for a school of medicine. As he explained, "Part of my life I spent caring for my parents. Another part I cared for my children. I have finally arrived at the time to care for myself. I have always dreamed of studying medicine. Now I want to realize my dream."

So I did some calculation. Eighty years. Imagining that if he passed the entrance exam, he would have six years of study before him. Completing school, he'd be 86 years old. Then it would be time for him to do residency. Two more years. Only at the age of 88 would be start to practice the medical profession.

My first impulse was to laugh at the insanity of an old man. Was it possible that he didn't know how to add up the years? Might he have no awareness of the limits of life?

But later, a gust of wisdom saved me. I smiled. And I thought, "Of course he knows all these things. Of course he knows that he probably won't have time enough to practice his profession. He knows that it's all useless. And despite all this, he's doing it. Useless like that tree that wasn't living for uses it might have. Rather, it was living for the joy of being."

Usefulness. Spoons, knives, brooms, pliers, hammers, toothpicks, combs, brushes: all useful. Their raison d'etre is that which can be done with them. They are tools, means, bridges, paths for things other than themselves. In themselves, they give neither pleasure nor joy to anyone.

Uselessness. The *Sonata* by Dominico Scarlatti on the harpsichord I listen to as I wrote this chronicle. The little poem by Emily Dickinson that I repeat by heart. The chalice of wine I drink. The nymphs of Monet over whom my eyes linger. The bonsai I take care of. The kite in the hand of a boy. The doll in the lap of a girl. The beloved hand that touches me. All these are good for nothing. They aren't useful tools for taking care of tasks. Nor are they paths or bridges. Whoever has these things has no need for tools, for with them, the desire to do desists. Whoever has these things does not need paths or bridges, for with them, the desire to go desists. There is no need to go because you've already arrived in the place of joy. Pleasure and joy reside in uselessness.

So I thought that that divine man was going to go to medical school in the way of one who writes a poem, or plays a sonata, or plants a bonsai, or flies a kite—for nothing other than the pure pleasure for the joy of being. I imagined that, perhaps, the joy of pleasure in uselessness was something that gods conceded to those who make peace with old age. For to them is given the grace, if they've become wise, of enjoying freedom from the compulsion of practicality—the terrible and mortal sickness that attacks young and old. All of those young and old want to be useful. All want to be tools. All want to live alongside knives, hammers, brooms, paths, and bridges.

Those who live under the compulsion of utility spend a lot of time working. And the whole time they are searching for something unreachable that is found after finishing a task, at the end of the path, on the other side of the bridge, a place which is always backing away.

Those who live in the grace of uselessness don't want to arrive anywhere. Because they have already arrived. I want to remain in the sonata, in the poem, in the wine, in the nymphs, in the bonsai, in the kite, in the doll, in the hand that touches me. That's why I love divine people, solitary trees on the hill, wood that cannot be used. I love them because they surrender themselves to crazy, useless acts—for the pure joy of being. I love that unknown Japanese immigrant who planted himself like a bonsai in an act by all appearances the poetic gesture of another divine man of the same race, Hokusai (1760-1849) as he approached the glorious age of 80. This is what he wrote:

> Since I was six years old I was obsessed with drawing the shape of things. By the age of 50, I had published an infinity of drawings. But everything I produced before the age of 70 isn't worth considering. At the age of 73, I learned a little about the true structure of the nature of animals, plants, birds, fish, and insects. Definitely by the age of 80 I will have made more progress. By 90, I will have penetrated the mystery of things. At 100, most

certainly, I will reach a wonderful phase, and when I'm 110, anything I do, be it a dot or a line, will be alive.

I see, high on the hill of Chang, not one tree but two. Their ages add up to 160 years. They talk and shake from laughing so much. They talk about the next 160 years...

Eternity

V

Wisdom

The Secret Garden

I am trying to understand how the rumor got started. It started, it spread, it was confirmed, and it became fact. When I try to take it back, they look at me with incredulous eyes. They are those patients who come for therapy...

[Here I must insert a parenthetical explanation, since I used a word that orthodoxy prohibits. I should not have said "therapy" but "analysis," as the analyst Bagé did. It is alleged that "analysis" is a scientific concept, a rigorous method employed by researchers who work in aseptic laboratory settings. Because this is exactly what they allege themselves to be doing: reducing the venomous neurotic and psychotic notions that make people crazy down to their simplest elements, with the objectivity of academic scholarship.

Therapy, on the other hand, is a modest word that lacks such dignity. In Greek, *therapeutés* is a "servant." The verb *therapeuein* means "care for," "take care of," as one would care for a garden, as one would take care of a child. Analysis belongs to the world of scholarship. Therapy belongs to the universe of compassion.]

... with precise expectations about that which awaits them. They hope that the therapist will lead them, like Dante, through the horrors of Hell and the terrors of Purgatory, because that's what is alleged to exist inside the Unconscious which we have heard spoken of. But they don't know the Unconscious at all. This expectation, preliminary to the adventure of self-knowledge, presupposes that the traveler believes that the territory to be visited, known as the "Unconscious." They believe it to be a kind of concentration camp of horrific, repulsive, reprehensible, ugly, stinking, disgusting scary things like the ones Bosch, Dalí, and Munch painted on their canvases.

Looking closely at Bosch's paintings, I was surprised by the similarity between the Christian unconscious and the psychoanalytic unconscious. The two are equally infernal. According to Dante, "Abandon all hope, ye who enter here." Is there anything more maddening than that?

This idea is not found in the Old Testament. The human soul is painted there with great tenderness. The Book of Ecclesiastes very much resembles Taoism. There is no vengeance to execute, no guilt to be expiated. The sinister unconscious is a theological thing of Christian churches, exemplified by the Dominican inquisitors and Calvinist theologians. For them, virtue and purity are no more than lies, superficial disguises that need to be unmasked to reveal that the Keinian feces and urine that fill the soul.[9] The Calvinists say: we are, by nature, totally depraved. There isn't the slightest grain of goodness in us. Beneath it all, there is always the devil's workshop. They therefore do not admire that the inquisitors had to validate themselves with fire and that we ourselves have had to construct, inside the body, a prison of stone and iron called the Unconscious, there to imprison our beastliness.

About priests, Blake said, "As the caterpillar seeks the most beautiful flowers to lay its eggs, so does the priest put his curses in our most beautiful joys." Bachelard said something like that about psychoanalysts. According to him, the psychoanalyst is that person who, upon seeing a flower, asks: "Where is the manure?" It's a technique of the confessional. The confessor soon suspects the penitent who speaks only of the garden. He will soon ask: "And in this beautiful garden, how many sins did you commit?"

The church learned of the unconscious through sin.

Psychoanalysis learned of the unconscious through neurosis and psychosis.

But there's another way: that of the poets. Poets come to know of the unconscious through Beauty. For them, the center of the unconscious is a garden. Someone shut it up, true enough. The key was lost. But it can be opened. And that is what Bachelard

---

[9] Melanie Klein (1882-1960) was a psychoanalyst who theorized that the adult unconscious is formed from existential anxiety in infancy, when the unconscious splits the world into good and bad idealizations.

proclaimed, inspired by the drawings of Chagall: "The universe—the drawings of Chagall prove it—has, despite all the other miseries, a destiny of happiness. Man should rediscover Paradise."

That's an old lesson. Diotima, the priestess who initiated Socrates in the secrets of love, told him that all men are pregnant with Beauty. Sooner or later this beauty will want to be born. A Sleeping Beauty lives within us, just as in the children's story and in the poem "Eros and Psyche" by Fernando Pessoa. Bachelard, who contemplated the unconscious (yes, contemplated! The unconscious is a silent scenario offered to enchanted eyes!) just as it reveals itself in candlelight, concluding: "Whoever trusts the fantasies of dim light will discover this psychological truth: the tranquil unconscious, free of nightmares, in equilibrium with its fantasies, is exactly the dark-light of the psyche, or, even better, the psyche of the dark-light. Images from the dim light teach us to like that dark-light of intimate vision"— the unconscious is a painting of a Flemish master.

In the artist's studio were born the sonatas of Beethoven, the paintings of money, the sculptures of Michelangelo, the poems of Fernando Pessoa, the Gregorian chant, the fairy tales, the religious myths. Toys, laughs, and joys are also made in that studio. It's a place of enchanted characters. There they are, as in dreams, the gnomes, Never-Never Land, the clowns, the Boy Jesus of Alberto Caeiro, and the playful monster Nietzsche.

But someone will have to be the midwife!

Someone will have to plant the kiss that breaks the spell! Someone will open the garden with the magic key!

Everything I am trying to say is said and seen in the film *The Secret Garden*. Its's about an allegory of the paths of the body and soul: how Beauty triumphs over Death. Being an allegory, the story that it tells is, at the same time, our own story. You will see yourself reflected in it just as Narcissus saw himself reflected in the spring. There is, inside us all, a closed "secret garden" that needs to be opened. The therapist, the servant, and the gardener. They are obligated to take care of the garden, to pull up the weeds and do away with the pests, for the flowers. Therapy is this: to visit the secret garden until the lost key is found.

Illness

I felt the fear in your voice on the telephone. You had discovered you were sick in a different way, as you never had been. There are ways to be sick, in accordance with the way of the sickness. Some illnesses are visitors: they arrive without warning, disturb the peace of the house, and then go. Such is the case of a broken leg, appendicitis, a cold, or measles. After a certain time, the illness packs its bags and says good-bye. And everything returns to the way it had always been.

Other illnesses come to stay. It's futile to complain. If they come to stay, you need to do with them what you would do if someone moved into your house forever: arrange the house as well as possible so that living together isn't painful. Who knows, but you might be able to take advantage of the situation.

You have already had several visiting illnesses. But your new one came to stay. Hypertension. 170 over 120. Very high. You have to bring it down to go on living. For this, there are little remedies that control the excesses of the intrusion. But to free yourself from it, cure it, apparently that is not possible. But it is possible to take advantage of the situation. I myself have lived with my hypertension for more than 20 years. And so far we haven't had any serious alteration.

Here's some advice: without playing at Pollyanna, treat your disease like a friend. More precisely: like a teacher that can make you wiser. Groddeck, one of the discoverers of Psychoanalysis whom almost no one remembers (which is a shame because he navigated through seas that most psychoanalysts don't know), said that illness isn't an invader that, coming from outside, penetrates the body forcefully. The opposite is true. It is a daughter of the body, a message generated in its depths and which blossoms into the surface of the flesh the same way that bubbles form in the depths of lakes to blossom and pop on the surface of the water. Illness has an initiating function: through it one can reach a greater knowledge of one's self. Illnesses are dreams in the form of physical suffering. So if you become a friend of your illness, it will give you free lessons about how to live more wisely.

It could be that you still haven't understood this, but the fact is, all of the beautiful things of the world are daughters of illness. Man created beauty as a remedy for illness, like a balm for his fear of dying. People who enjoy perfect health don't create anything. If we depended on them, the world could be a dull sameness. Why have they had to create? Creation is the fruit of suffering.

"To think is to be sick in the eyes," said Alberto Caeiro. The eyes of the poet had to be sick because if they weren't, the world would be poorer and uglier because the poem would not have been written.

Because Alberto Caeiro's eyes were sick, a poem was written and, through it, we have the joy of reading what the poet wrote. The body produces beauty to live with a disease.

To believe the poet Heine, it was to cure his infirmity that God created the world. God created the world because he was love-sick.... That's why God said, according to the poet: "The illness was the source of my impulse and my creative strength; creating, I convalesced; creating, I became healthy again."

Thinking about why a painful experience of illness had passed, Nietzsche said this:

> ...this is how, now, that long period of illness appeared to me: I feel as if through it I had again discovered life, even discovered myself. I tried all the good things, even the small things, in a way that others had not easily tried them. And so I transformed my will to health and to live into a philosophy.

Illness is the possibility of loss, and emissary of death. At its touch, everything becomes fluid, evanescent, ephemeral. People you love, your children—they all take on the iridescent beauty of a soap bubble. Meanings reached through the possibility of loss awaken from their lethargy. Banal objects, ignored, suddenly become luminous. If we knew that we were going to go blind, what scenes we would see in a simple grain of sand! Who ever feels pleasure in simple quotidian wonder of not feeling pain? I came to understand this in an almost ecstasy of mystic gratitude when, after a few centuries of the intolerable pain of renal colic (the pain always lasts centuries), the wizard Dolantina returned me to the amazing condition of not feeling pain. Health dulls the senses. Illness resuscitates them.

So don't fight with your illness. It has come to stay. Try to learn what it wants to teach you. It wants you to be wise. It wants to resuscitate your sleeping feelings. It wants to give you the sensibility of artists. All artists, without exception, are sick... You need to turn yourself into an artist. You will be more beautiful. As you become more beautiful, you will be more loved. And being more loved, you will become happy.

Mental Health

I was invited to give a lecture about mental health. The people who invited me supposed that I, as a psychoanalyst, ought to be a specialist in the subject. And I thought so, too. So much so that I accepted. But as soon as I stopped and thought about it, I regretted it. I saw that I didn't know anything. Let me explain.

I began my thoughts by making a list of people who, in my point of view, have had a rich and exciting mental life, people whose books and projects are food for my soul. Nietzsche, Fernando Pessoa, Van Gogh, Wittgenstein, Cecília Meireles, Vladimir Mayakovski. And then I was shocked. Nietzsche went crazy. Fernando Pessoa was given to drink. Van Gogh killed himself. Wittgenstein was happy to know he would die soon; he no longer tolerated living with such angst. Cecília Meireles suffered chronic light depression. Mayakovski committed suicide. All of them were profound, lucid people who will continue to be bread for the living long after we have been completely forgotten.

But did they have mental health? Mental health, that condition in which ideas behave themselves, always balanced, foreseeable, without surprises, obedient to the commands of duty, everything in it places like soldiers in rank order, never allowing the body to miss work or do something unexpected. It isn't necessary to take a trip around the world in a sailboat. It's enough to do what Shirley Valentine did. (If you haven't seen tat eponymous film yet, do.) Or have a prohibited love affair, or, more dangerous than all of this, the courage to think what's never been thought. Thinking is a dangerous thing...

No, mental health they did not have. They were too lucid for that. They knew that the world is controlled by crazy old people in neckties. Being owners of power, the crazy go on to become the prototypes of mental health. Of course none of the names I cited would survive the tests that psychologists would have subjected them to if they were to look for employment in a company. On the other hand, I've never heard of a politician who had stress or depression. They always go parading around the streets of town, passing out smiles and certainties.

I feel like my thoughts are the thoughts of a crazy person, so let me hurry on to some obligatory clarifications.

We are very much like computers. The function of the computer, as everybody knows, requires the interaction of two parts. One of them is called hardware, literally the hard equipment, and the other is called software. The hardware consists of all the solid things that the appliance is made of. The software is made up of "spiritual" entities—symbols that form the programs and are recorded on discs.

We, too, have hardware and software. The hardware are the nerves of the brain, the neurons, all that that makes up the nervous system. The software is made up of a series of applications that are recorded in our memory. Just as in computers, what remains in the memory are symbols, gossamer-light entities that could be said to be "spiritual," the most important application being language.

A computer can go crazy through a flaw in its hardware or its software. So can we. When our hardware goes crazy, we call in the psychiatrists and neurologists, who come in with their chemical potions and scalpels to fix what went bad. When the problem is in our software, however, potions and scalpels don't work. You can't fix an application with a screwdriver. Since software is made of symbols, only symbols can get into it. To deal with software, you have to make use of symbols. For that reason, whoever deals with disturbances in human software never sees anything good in physical resources. Their tools are words, and they may be poets, humorists, clowns, writers, gurus, friends, or even psychoanalysts.

It happens, though, that this computer that is the human body has a peculiarity that differentiates it from others. Its hardware, the body, is sensitive to things that the software produces. And isn't that what happens to us? We hear a song and we cry. We read Drummond's erotic poems and the body gets excited.

Imagine a sound system. Imagine that the record player and accessories, the hardware, had the capacity to hear the music that it played and to be emotionally moved. And imagine that the beauty is so great that the hardware doesn't behave and beaks down with emotion! Well that's what happened with those people I cited at the beginning. The music that came out of their software was so beautiful that their hardware couldn't stand it.

Given these theoretical presuppositions, we are now in a position to offer a recipe that will guarantee, for those who accept the risk, mental health until the end of their days.

Opt for modest software. Avoid beautiful and emotionally moving things. Beauty is dangerous to hardware. Be careful with music. Brahms and Mahler are especially contraindicated. Rock can be taken at will. As for readings, avoid those that make you think. There is a vast literature specializing in impeding thought. If there are books by Dr. Lair Ribeiro[10], why risk reading Saramago? Newspapers have the same effect. They should be read daily. Since they publish the same things every day with different names and faces, it is guaranteed that our software will always think the same things. And on Sundays, don't forget Silvio Santos and Gugu Liberato[11].

Following this recipe, you will have a banal but tranquil life. But since you have cultivated insensibility, you will not sense how banal it is. And instead of reaching the end that the people I mention reached, you will retire to realize your dreams. Unfortunately, however, when you arrive at that moment, you will have forgotten what they were.

---

[10] Brazilian cardiologist and internationally renowned author of self-help books for executives.

[11] Silvio Santos is the Brazilian host of a gaudy Sunday television program of pop culture. Liberato was his producer and also a television personality.

The Rat Gnawed the King's Cheese

I was lying down, reading a story to my granddaughter Mariana when, all of a sudden, I had a mystical experience of illumination. I saw, with a clarity beyond any doubt, something which the most rigorous philosophers have never managed to see. I saw, as if in a painting, the solution to the enigma of democracy.

There was once in a distant country a king who loved cheese above any other pleasure. His love of cheese was so great that, motivated by scientific curiosity and gastronomic interest, he sent for the most renowned cheese specialists in all the world. He offered them resources not only to continue the making of cheeses already known but also to dedicate themselves to research into new cheeses, thus to widen the frontiers of science, technology, and gastronomy. Cheeses made with whale milk and unicorn milk would become famous for their aphrodisiacal virtues.

The king's palace was an enormous depository of cheeses of all types, among them camembert, cheddar, edam, Emmental, gorgonzola, gouda, limburger, parmesan, pecorino, provolone, sapsago, Trappista, *prato*, *minas*, mozzarella, and ricotta, among others.

The country became famous and grew rich with the exportation of cheeses. Its aroma crossed the seas. Universities were created with the objective of developing the science of cheese. There was even a technical school that, under the rigors of the exegesis of the Holy Scripture, concluded that the sacrament of the eucharist was originally celebrated not with bread and wine but with wine and cheese, from which came the custom that continues today in more profane celebrations.

Meanwhile, it happened that besides the king and the people there were other beings in the kingdom who also liked cheese: rats. Attracted by the smell that issued from the palace, they moved there by the thousands immediately went to the banquet of royal cheeses.

The rats took over the place. They were in the cabinets, the drawers, the canisters, the beds, the sofas, in the kitchen, in hats and shoes and bags and even in the king's beard.

But worst of all was that the rats, endowed with digestive imperatives, had to expel through one end what they had swallowed at the other, and wherever they went, they left in the corridors, the salons and bedrooms of the palace an immense trail of little turds, round, hard, and smelly.

Furious, the king called his ministers and asked them: "What can we do to free ourselves from the rats?" And they responded, "Easy, Your Majesty. Just bring in some cats."

The king was overjoyed with the brilliant idea. He sent for a hundred cats to put an end to the rats.

The rats, upon seeing the cats, fled in terror. Away went the rats; there stayed the cats. They filled the palace. Just like the rats, the cats at everything they saw, and, driven by the same physiological demands that had driven the rodents, covered the shiny floors of the palace with their malodorous poop.

Furious, the king called in his ministers and asked them, "What can we do to free ourselves from the cats?" And they responded, "Easy, Your Majesty. Just bring in some dogs. In came dogs of all sorts—large, small, short, long, smooth and speckled.

The cats, upon seeing the dogs, fled in terror. Away went the cats; there stayed the dogs. They filled the palace. And the same old story happened again. Dog-do all over the place.

The king was furious. He called his ministers together and asked them, "What do we do to free ourselves from these dogs?"

And they responded, "Your Majesty, it's easy. Bring in some lions."

In came the lions with their manes and their roars. As soon as the dogs saw them, they fled, tails between their legs. Away went the dogs; there stayed the lions. But the lions didn't just eat a hundred times more; they also pooped a hundred times more than the minuscule mutts. The royal treasury was in crisis. The gold reserves dropped. There wasn't enough money for meat and to pay the poop-picker-uppers, who threatened to go on strike.

The king was furious. He called his ministers together and asked them, "What can we do to free ourselves from the lions?" And they responded, "It's easy, Your Majesty. Just bring in some elephants."

Away went the lions; there stayed the elephants. They ate mountains and pooped mountains. The palace turned into a huge mountain of elephant shit. And the kingdom's stink crossed o'er the seas.

The king was furious. He called his ministers together and asked, "What can we do to free ourselves from the elephants?"

The ministers then remembered that the elephants. who feared almost nothing, trembled with fear upon sight of a mouse.

And the ministers responded in chorus, "It's easy, Your Majesty. Just bring in some rats!"

And thus it was done. They went back to the rats. Away went the elephants, and everyone lived happily ever after.

The day will come when my granddaughter will have grown. I will not longer tell her stories. She will learn about politics. She will want to visit the buildings of the National Congress, symbols of democracy. She will notice that there are mouse droppings everywhere. Shocked, she will tell me, "Grandpa, there must be a lot of rats around here!" And I will respond, "Yes, many are the rats."

And she will ask me, "But why don't they bring in some cats to get rid of the rats?" And then I will tell her the story again, and I will tell her: "Learn the big lesson of democracy. Better the droppings of a rat than an elephant."

The Gift

It is indisputable common knowledge that gifts are the bearers of happiness. That's why we give them to people we love: to make them happy.

Settling onto this premise, the logic of my thinking was impeccable since the rule of three doesn't let us go wrong. "If a gift contains a quantum 'X,' 20 gifts will contain 20 times more happiness."

Common sense and the rule of three have convinced me: each of those transparent little bags, with 20 balloons in many colors in each, contains 20 times more happiness than one lone balloon of one color. So I took two from the store shelf and bought them.

It all started a week before. I was a guest in the house of a friend in the United States. It was Halloween, and we had just come back from a party with his son and daughter, six and seven years old, respectively, two charming children. Each of them held a fluttering ballon. So, what was going to happen sooner or later happened sooner. One of their balloons hit the branch of a bush, and it burst with a pop. And then the crying. Not because of the balloon but because of symmetry. What hurt was the fact that one had a balloon and the other didn't.

What hurts isn't the absence of something but the fact of someone else having it and we don't. If neither if neither of us has it, the absence doesn't hurt. I tried to console the girl. Told her that the next day I was going on a trip, but I'd be back within a week, and when I came back, I'd try to bring a bigger, better balloon.

Returning form my trip, headed for my friend's house, I was getting ready to fulfill my promise. It's just that, instead of one balloon, I was taking 20. Instead of balloons only for the boy, balloons for him and his sister. Instead of balloons the size of the one that burst, balloons even bigger. Instead of a balloon of one color, balloons of many colors. There I went, a world of happiness in my suitcase.

I arrived at night. The children were sleeping. When they woke up the next day—it was a Sunday—I heard from the noise of the television that the two were already up. Up and content.

Happy without gifts. Children are like that: they need little to be happy. I thought: it's time to multiply their happiness!

I went to the TV room, packages held hidden. "Do you remember what I promised?" I asked. They didn't remember. They'd already forgotten what had happened on Halloween.

Half-disappointed, I gave them the little packages of balloons and went back to my room, convinced I had done something good. The climate went back to the tranquility of before. But not for long. I soon heard shouts and gripes. I ran to the TV room. The two were wrestling around. All because of the balloons. One of the packages had just one white balloon while the other had three. The one who had gotten three white balloons felt cheated, since it was believed that the white balloons were uglier than the colored ones. I intervened with authority. I took the balloons back. I took out the four white balloons from the 40. Thirty-six remained. I gave each of them 18. I re-established symmetry. Peace returned. I then understood that giving a gift is an art that requires a deep understanding of the human soul.

Presents aren't packages of happiness, as the innocent think. Presents are magical entities. Whoever gives a gift is doing "a job." Presents are curses that awaken sleeping powers of the human soul.

Of all those curses, the most powerful is that of "comparison." Comparison is the serpent's egg from which envy is born. The boy and the girl were happy with their old toys. I gave them a new gift. The new gift poisoned their eyes, which began to make comparisons. From that surged envy and strife.

It's easy to break the spell. All you have to do is not look at someone else's present. But some presents are given only to provoke looks of envy, the one's that say, "mine is more, mine is bigger than yours." A diamond ring is given to be shown off. Of course I believe you gave it out of pure love. But that moment of romantic rapture, accompanied with a little wine, candles, and declarations of eternal love, doesn't last long. A little while later the ring goes on to circulate in another circuit: the the circuit of others' eyes, where larger and smaller rings are found. The nice thing about rings is in their provocation of envy.

Why would the man give a diamond ring? Each ring, destitute of any practical significance, is an exhibition of economic excess that, after all due symbolic transformations, can understood as an exhibition of phallic exuberance. "Ah! How potent your husband is!" the envious women will say when they see your ring. This also belongs to the chapter on male sexuality. But since it wouldn't be right for a discrete executive to directly open his peacock tail, he uses the woman for that purpose. Look closely and you will see inside the diamond ring an arrogant husband.

Children know this quite well. After the initial enthusiasm over Christmas presents, they do the accounting. They "count" the presents they got. They already know that part of their happiness isn't in the presents themselves but in having received more than the others. It's sad to know that in the middle of the apparent happiness with the presents is the sinister movement of eyes known as envy, which feeds itself on the destruction of joy. When you get ready to buy Christmas presents, watch out for the curse...

I Did Not Travel

The color of my skin is as it has always been. I didn't get a tan on a beach. I didn't take a plane to the Caribbean or the Northeast of Brazil, nor to the South. I stayed home. I could have gone, but I preferred to say. I stayed without feeling envy of the pleasures of those who went somewhere. Many people travel, not because they want to but because they see everyone else going, and they can't stand to stay, imagining that the others are drinking coconut milk, eating shrimp, and having a crazy-good time. I stayed without envy. I didn't want to travel. At least I didn't want to travel from one place to another. I wanted to delight myself with the pleasures at hand. At home. There are trips that can only be made inside. To do so, one must stay.

The philosopher Karl Jaspers says that he never traveled. He alleged, with philosophical arrogance, that in his house everything worth knowing could be found. Philosophical arrogance and psychoanalytic foolishness. I never saw anything so foolish justified. I think he didn't travel because he feared traveling. Accustomed to an entire life of nothing but reading, when he arrived at a beautiful place, he didn't know what to do.

Like St. George, who trained for his entire life to fight the dragon. But he never killed because if he did, he would end up with nothing to do. So St. George, one nice day, in armor, on horseback with lance, goes to the daily fight. Once he gets there, he finds the beautiful impassioned fair damsel, who explains, "Oh, Georgie! You know that prince who turned into a frog because of a witch's spell? Well I, a princess, am going to turn into a dragon because of a curse. But now that a thousand years have passed, the spell has broken. Come on, Georgie, with your other lance, your lance of love..." Her saying that was enough for St. George's lance to be stricken with sudden softness, and it curled up into a cooked noodle. Sometimes it is easier to fight a dragon than to make love with a fair maiden in love.

Well that's how the poor philosopher was. Used to seeing everything through books, he was horrified to be face-to-face with the thing itself. I imagine that in his few frustrating travel experiences, he stayed in his room in the hotel, re-reading *Kritik der Reinen Vernunft*, terrified to go out and perambulate down unknown alleys. For the philosopher, only that which can be turned into a book is real.

Karl Jaspers was wrong when he said that everything worth knowing could be found in his house. I don't travel to learn. I travel for pleasure. I think I'll learn more about Michelangelo by staying at home and reading books about him that by going to Florence. But when I go to Florence, my imagination flies and, when I walk down the streets, I imagine that he, too, walked them. It's that magical sensation of...what exactly? No, it isn't contemporaneity, to be in a same time, because centuries separate us. It's "con-spaciality"—a word that does not exist. I just looked for it in the *Aurélio* dictionary. But it should exist and, for that reason, I invented it. It's a feeling like that of the Goethe character, writing to his lover, saying, "No, I don't have anything to say. I am writing to you because I know your hands will touch this sheet of paper..." And this: the mystic joy of sharing the same space despite the distance in time.

I think the philosopher's justification is foolish, but there's a hint of reason. There are people who travel the whole world, by plane, without ever disembarking from the banal and mediocre village of their soul. They see everything but look at nothing. They return no larger than before, the same way as before without having become more beautiful, with no greater shine in their eyes, a shine like a rainbow. Because they come back empty inside and bearing bad smells.

To travel well, a passport, money and tickets aren't enough. Because, as Bernardo Soares said, "We never disembark from ourselves. Do they think they are seeing the world? They're fooling themselves. "What we see isn't what we see; we see ourselves." Every photo, every story about the trip is a revelation of our interior scenes. Soares continues: "Carlyle said, 'Any road, even this road from Entepfuhl, takes you to the end of the world.' But the road from Entepfuhl, if followed all the way, even to the end, returns to Entepfuhl in such a way that Entepfuhl, where we've already been, is that same end of the world that we set out to find." And, "Whoever crossed the seas crossed only his own boredom with himself." Boredom is not cured by travel. One cures oneself at home. "What can China give me that my soul hasn't already given me? And, if my soul can't give it to me, how will China give it to me? If it's with my soul I see China, will I see it?" And, "We are eternal transients through ourselves; there is no landscape other than ourselves."

It's a trip too short. This time, I decided to travel by staying. So many books that I haven't seen. *The Most Beautiful Book of the Italian Kitchen:* if someday I return to Italy, the dishes will never have the same flavor since I've tasted of this wonderful book. And the books on art, the paintings of Chagall, Kandisky, Klimt, Monet, Miró, Bosch. The CDs that I have bought and not yet had time to listen to. And the delight of writing—something I can't do when I travel. Those who don't know think that inspiration comes when one travels to wonderful places. Total mistake. When what you see if wonderful, the thinker stops thinking. He or she is happy just to make love with what is seen. Standing before a Monet painting, I think absolutely nothing. I just look. Only critics think, because (poor things!) they are obliged to have opinions on everything. But I'm not like that. I don't need to have opinions. When I travel, I don't want to have thoughts; I want to have sensations. I want to give the thinker a vacation.

My thought was a wish to write. I've already thought a lot. It was time to give birth. So I stayed in my micro-world to give birth. Until the pain could give pleasure. This is the good thing about having learned to play with thought: one travels a lot, without moving from place. That was it. I stayed and I traveled.

It's in Talking that We Misunderstand

It's early morning, that confusing interlude between being asleep and being awake, when the gods give me their revelations. So it happens that the more banal things appear before me from behind, which takes me by surprise because, from behind, things are the opposite of what they seem to be from the front.

Today, for example, the gods revealed to me that separation comes from understanding. For us to be together, it's best not to understand. This is the opposite of what couples think when they live in constant argument. They think their fights are because they don't understand each other, so they ask therapists for help, because who knows, maybe the therapist will help them understand each other better, which is a fact, but the conclusion doesn't follow from the premise. It isn't certain that after they understand each other they'll remain together.

Often it's at the precise moment of understanding that separation becomes inevitable. Nothing guarantees that understanding will be nice. The proof of this is what happened to my father-in-law, who hated brain. Invited to a dinner, he tasted a wonderful breaded cauliflower, enjoyed it, helped himself to seconds, and filled himself right up with it. After the meal, he complimented the hostess on the divine dish. But then she explained: "It isn't cauliflower, it's breaded brain..." —and he understood. And the understanding catapulted him in the direction of the nearest bathroom, where he heaved up the meal. That's how it is. Sometimes, when people don't understand something, they eat and enjoy. When they understand, they get disgusted and vomit.

Backwards statements like that, so contrary to common sense, demand an explanation—and that's what I'm coming around to do by means of a long curve which, in non-Euclidean geometry, is the shortest distant between two points.

In my computer I opened a file with the name "Encyclicals." There I put the text of encyclicals that I will promulgate when I am elected pope. As you know, Pope Leo XIII, in 1891, promulgated the encyclical *De Rerum Novarium*, which means "On New Things." All of a sudden, the Church, which until then had believed that everything worth knowing was stored in its millennial chest of doctrines, understood, with fright, that extremely new and interesting things were happening in the world.

And the good pope hurried to pass this information on. This was the beginning of an enormous modernization effort by the church that didn't work out because you don't put a patch of new cloth on old cloth. The old cloth had just started to tear... Wishing to repair the bad done by the *De Rerum Novarum* caused, I wrote its antithesis, the encyclical *De Rerum Vetustarum*, or "On Old Things."

Its substance is extraordinarily simple. The encyclical prays that, from the moment of its publication, everything, absolutely everything that happens in the Church—the liturgies, the priestly blessings, the baptisms, the christenings, weddings, funerals, hymns, readings of the Holy scripture, sermons, encyclicals, and even the words of the father in the confessional—everything would have to be done in Latin. Oh! How beautiful Latin is! It sounds like pure music, a "liturgy of crystal."

Music is poetry at its highest point, when the words completely lose any meaning and transform into pure beauty, beauty that doesn't look for meanings. Ineffable beauty without words. There can be no squabbles over music. So, if everything in the Church happened in Latin, it would be as if it were only music—there would be no possibility of misunderstandings.

If the priests and the bishops spoke in Latin, we wouldn't understand anything, and we would love everything. Because music is like that: we love it without understanding it. The Oracle of Delphi, wise and clever, knew that quite well and never said anything that others understood. Clear, distinct language kills fantasy. She spoke her enigmas, pure music, in strange language. It isn't by chance that the Pentecostals and Charismatics grow the way they do: by the power of strange language that no one understands. Everything fits inside that which no one understands: brain turns to cauliflower, and the body and mind approve.

I would really like to visit a monastery where speaking prose is prohibited—where only poetry is read and stories told and music heard: Gregorian chants, Bach, the saxophone of Jan Garbarek, the piano of Keith Jarrett, the *Carmina Burana*, Jean-Pierre Rampal playing Japanese melodies, Maurice André and his trumpet... Or a Quaker congregation where silence is nurtured, no one speaks, everyone listens, the voice of God heard only when everyone is quiet.

Understanding always causes fights. I really imagine that's why God confused the language of humanity in the construction of the Tower of Babel. People spoke the same language. Speaking, they understood each other. Understanding each other, they understood each others' opinions. Understanding each others' opinions, they didn't like each other. Then came the fights. God All-Powerful then understood that the only way to avoid fighting was to make it so they couldn't understand each other. And thus was born music, the language that no one understands and everyone loves.

It's in talking that we misunderstand each other. At some future moment, I will continue my torturous wanderings, passing the church, the place where eternal marriages are blessed, to arrive at home, the place where we know that marriages are ephemeral. For now, I stick with my advice for couples who are fighting. Be careful with talk. From talk understanding can be born, from understanding separation can happen. Understanding can be as fatal for marriage as it was for my father-in-law's dinner. It's in talk that we misunderstand each other.

Avoid marriage counseling. It can lead to intolerable understanding. Understanding can lead to insanity. There are insanities that can result from clarity of thought. Adopt the millennial wisdom of the Church: adopt Latin as the language of your house. And dedicate yourselves to music, with preference for wind instruments, because while you're blowing in them, you can't talk, and thus understanding and separations are avoided.

Sad Song

I understand my friends' concern There was even a dear friend who was so worried that she brought me a wonderful bottle of Jack Daniels, elixir of the Dionysian gods She was cure that the powers of that liquid would return to me the joy that seemed lost. Well, that's what my friends thought, that joy had abandoned me.

It didn't help that I had written two essays about masculine sexuality which were just playing around with a painful truth. If they had paid attention, they would have become a little wiser and come to understand that the soul is well not when everything else is well. to the customary greeting, "Hey, all well, all calm?" I always answer, "Not even for God the All-powerful, is all well and calm." The soul is well when it can dance on he shoulders of the Devil.

Contrary to the friend that gave me the Jack Daniels, I know from indirect means about a person who decided not to write to me anymore, alleging that I was depressed. I was very offended because this means that I am a bottle of Sleinad Kcaj, a drink you have never seen on any shelf of imported booze, unless you have to have seen Jack Daniels reflected in a mirror, since that's exactly what this name, which looks more like a Croatian word, is. Jack Daniels backwards. Or, if the former is a bottle of joy and levity, Sleinad Kcaj—me, my essays—is a bottle of sadness.

I counter-attack with a verse by Adélia Prado, who has a soul that seems a lot like mine. "Sad song, the one who can deal with it never lost joy." Want more? "By the pleasure of sadness I live happily." Want more? "Love is a happiest thing; love is the saddest thing; love is the thing I most want."

I have real terror of cheerful, the life of the party, where everyone is obligated to be happy. How tiring, what a vexation for the spirit! What the cheerful like most is beer and a little cheese, a nice thing that I myself enjoy. But I don't eat food to ward off beauty. The cheerful neither generate nor stop beauty. The cheerful can stand a sunset. As soon as they see it, their eyes and soul are upset. They wander off to make some noise, rile things up, and say that it's happiness—happy hour—when it's really just fear of silence.

But what a lousy soul is the one that is so gelatinous that it can't stand a vision of beauty? There is therapy for depression. So I'm going to invent a therapy for cheerfulness. And it's gong to be a Lacanian moment.[12] The session will be finished only when they cry. They are going to listen to Beethoven and Mahler to stop being so gelatinous and to learn of the strength that exists in sadness. And they're going to have to go through van Gogh and Monet to understand the lessons of time, for whoever is afraid of sadness is also afraid of time. And through Cecília Meireles and Robert Frost so they can feel good in autumn and evening.

Whoever can't befriend sadness is a candidate for a psychiatric consultation and a diet of antidepressants and tranquilizers. Whoever makes peace with sadness also learns about beauty because the two are always together. The Jews were right in their Easter rituals, mixing bitter herbs with food. Because life is like that.

Vincius de Morães said that he wanted to weep before beauty. Adélia Prado also said that beautiful fills the eyes with

---

[12] Jacque Lacan, controversial French psychoanalyst and psychiatrist who wrote of, among many other things, the depression that can follow jubilation.

water. The Beatles had that ballad where they say, "Because the sky is blue, it makes me cry." I cry to read poetry. I cry to hear music. I cry when I see a painting. And my soul is fine and don't want to be any different. Can you imagine the absurdity of me no longer looking at the blue sky, at the setting sun, at the works of art, in order to avoid crying? Let me repeat Adélia: "For the pleasure of sadness I live happily." Beauty is the pleasure of sadness.

You don't understand why one cries before beauty? The answer is simple. When it contemplates beauty, the soul beseeches eternity. Everything you love you wish would remain forever. But everything you love exists under the march of time. *Tempus fugit.* all is ephemeral. The sunset is ephemeral; the song is ephemeral; the hug is ephemeral, the house you build for the rest of your life is ephemeral.

We cry before beauty because beauty is a metaphor of life itself. that's why we imagine the gods. After all, what are the gods if not powers that will make beloved lost things return? When the heart says, "May beauty be eternal!"–at that exact moment a god is born. So don't get upset. My soul is fineIt can handle a sad song. I go around singing an old song, now forgotten, by Denoy de Oliveira and Ferreira Gullar: "Since two and two make four, I know that life is worthwhile."

My "depressing" essays obey the structure of a Beethoven sonata called *Les Adieux*. The first part is a sad adagio that starts off with three chords that sadly say, *"Lebewohl!" (Adeus)*. The second, *camminata expressivs,* is *Absence*. But the last, *vivacemente*, exulting in joy, is *Das Wiedersehen, the Return*.

Relax, relax... At the moment, I'm still on *Lebewohl*. Soon enough I'll get to *Das Wiedersehen*.

VI

LOVE

To Lovers, with Care...

A distressed reader wrote to me asking me to help her, in that I was the unwitting cause of her suffering. Her reading of a book I wrote, *The Girl and the Enchanted Bird*, had caused her great disturbance because of things I said there through the beak of a bird. I wrote there that longing helps love for it is in the pain of separation that the heart does its magic act of re-enchanting the loves that daily life had made plain. That was why the bird, after a time of hugs and petting, said that it was time to leave, because without longing—his as much as the girl's—they would lose their enchantment, and their love would end.

I imagine my reader must have had an opinion like that of the girl, who in some way agreed with the bird's reasoning, which led her to the crazy act of buying a silver cage where she locked up the sleeping bird, thinking that they'd live an endless honeymoon. Anyone who has read the book knows the end, and anyone who hasn't should buy a copy. Well the reader asked me if longing is necessary for love to grow.

Longing is a painful hole in the soul. The presence of an absence. One knows that something is missing. A piece of us was torn away. Everything turns bad. Longing becomes an aura that surrounds us. Wherever we go, it goes, too. Everything makes us remember the beloved person. Everything that's beautiful becomes sad, since beauty without the beloved is always sad. That's when people learn what it means to love: the desire for the re-encounter that will bring back happiness.

Longing is a lot like hunger. Hunger is also an emptiness. The body knows that something is missing. Hunger is the longing of the body. Longing is the hunger of the soul.

Now imagine that you are nuts about shrimp. Just speaking about shrimp makes your mouth water. Driven by the hunger for shrimp, you decide to eat shrimp for a month. You go out and buy 50 kilos of the large ones, and you eat shrimp for lunch and dinner. In the beginning, it's a party. "Shrimp à la Bahiana," "Shrimp à la Greek," "Stuffed shrimp." "Shrimp Milanese," shrimp stew with manioc," "risotto à la shrimp," "shrimp à la squash." Well I guarantee you that your hunger for shrimp will not last a week. At the end of the first week, just the smell of shrimp will set your stomach into convulsions, and what you are really going to want is rice, beans, chayote, tomato and beefsteak with fries.

There's a saying that says that the best food is porridge with hunger. An old friend of mine was lost in the Sierra del Mar for three days. His private plane had crashed on the mountain. For three days he had nothing to eat. He and his friend finally arrived at the house of a peasant way out in the woods. The only thing the woman had was cornmeal, which she made into a porridge. Well when the porridge was ready, Miguelzinho—for that was his name—didn't even wait for a spoon. He stuck his hand into the middle of that wonderful delicacy, so worthy of the gods, and stuffed himself. That's why Adélia, wise poetess, prayed to the almighty God: "I want neither knife nor cheese; what I want is hunger." Longing is hunger. Where there's hunger, gruel is delicious. Where there's longing, love is delicious.

So I advised her: If you have ideas like those of the little girl in the story and plan to cage your bird so you'll never long for it, in the illusion that love can live off kisses and hugs, get rid of that notion. Kisses and hugs are like shrimp: delicious and exciting. But if served every day, they're nauseating.

You invoke the fox from *The Little Prince* against me, since she says that longing has meaning only if you know when the beloved person will return. If you know when, the ritual of waiting begins. This is very true and very good. But I'm going to invoke Chico against the fox: "Longing is the opposite of birth. Longing is straightening up the bedroom of a child who has died." The child will never return. All that remains is longing as a manifestation of love. The bedroom that you clean up is a rite of love, knowing that the beloved person will never return.

My dear friend: unfortunately, love is made of many "nevermores"—the saddest expression there is.

So then you jump from the bird to the frog, asking me if, should the frog not turn into a prince at first kiss, one should insist on a great big kiss. Some observations are appropriate here.

First: Any prince who is subjected to a diet of shrimp sans surcease turns into a frog.

Second: There are frogs who are resistant to kissing. Proof of this is in the story of the little princess who let a ball of gold fall into a pond, a ball her father had given her as a gift (the king was crazy, with no discretion at all). Hearing his girl cry, an enormous frog with bugged eyes came out of the water and said that he would give her the ball of gold if she would agree to sleep with him. Even today frogs say the same thing to foolish girls, only today they don't say "sleep with" but "hook up with." The girl agreed, but as soon as she had the ball she ran off, leaving behind the frog and all his hopping around. But the frog did not give up. He went to the palace, called the king, told him what had happened, and the king, crazy and without discretion as we already pointed out, obliged the girl to sleep with the frog. If it were today, no doubt she'd run off to a night club. When the frog approached her, she was so sickened that she grabbed him by a leg and threw him against a wall. She backed off. When the frog hit the ground, he turned into a handsome prince. And that's how it goes:

there are frogs who turn into princes when they are thrown against a wall. Try it.

Third: If, after the spell of kisses and throwing the frog against a wall the frog goes on being a frog, it's because he really is a frog. No spell will solve the problem.

In this case, the only solution is for you to turn into a frog. Because, if you were a frog, you would think your frog a marvelous prince. Then you would have a lot of little frogs.

You asked me what to do when the heart firmly believes that the frog is a prince and the frog says that he really is a frog, genetically, not by option. What to do? I think you need to distrust your heart. The heart is great for loving. But for that very reason its opinions aren't reliable. Many people firmly believe that the sun revolves around the Earth and that nazism is wonderful. It could be that the frog is telling the truth.

The advantage of the frog is that he will never flap his wings like a bird. Many people prefer frogs to birds. Frogs are more reliable. People always know where they will be: in the swamp. But birds—where will they be? It's so painful to see them getting ready to depart!

The advantage of birds over frogs is that they are more beautiful: wild and indomitable creatures.

A question: Why don't you stop being the girl and turn yourself into the bird? Flap your wings. Leave the frog waiting. Like Shirley Valentine. Who knows what spells will occur? You still haven't tested the power of longing on the heart of frogs. It just might work.

Tenderness

. . . and all of a sudden I awoke, too early, for no reason whatsoever. I looked at the alarm clock. Four o'clock in the morning. My body said I should sleep a little more so I don't get sleepy during the day. But notions in my head demanded that I play with them. I tried oriental meditation, emptying my head of all thoughts. According to Taoism, we awaken because there are thoughts in our mind that demand to be thought. If we empty the head of such thoughts, we will return to sleep.

To stop thinking, all you have to do is do what this verse says: "The sound of water is exactly what I am thinking." If what I think is the sound of water, then it isn't my thought; it's the sound of water. The sound of water, without thoughts, puts one to sleep. There was no sound of water. But there was the tick-tock of the clock. I tried to practice the Taoist technique. I repeated: "The tick-tock of the clock says exactly what I am thinking." It was futile. There was an image that wanted to play with me—aside from just wanting to wake me up. And the image was so beautiful that I could not resist...

A painting by a Flemish painter, a specialist in subtlety of light and shadow. A woman, sunk in the dark of a bedroom, holds a candle in her left hand. Her face shines, lit by the warm light of the flame. In her right hand, which the candle light turns almost transparent, she protects the flame, which trembles and leans, blown by a breeze. Is she opening the door for someone, at that hour of the night? That would explain the leaning of the flame in the wind as much as her smile. A smile, in its own way, is also a flame that trembles at the waft of a breeze. This image makes me feel tenderness. Tenderness is a weak, fragile feeling. Like the flame. It needs fragility to survive. The word itself says so. The word *Tenderness* derives from *tender*, meaning "soft." The tender is tenuous. It never claws.

But the flame, fragile, can start fires. Tomás, the doctor in *The Unbearable Lightness of Being*, was a man of many lovers whom he systematically returned to their homes at the end of the night after their pleasure. With Tereza, it was different. She showed up unexpectedly. She had nowhere to sleep. She went to Tomás's apartment. She was burning with fever. He had no way to take her home the way he did with others. Kneeling at his headboard, it occurred to him that she had come to him like a basket on the waters. Anyone who arrives in a basket on the waters can only be a baby. Because of this tender image, he fell in love with her. Oh, what a beautiful picture Tomás could have painted if, instead of being a doctor, he were a painter.

Tenderness distinguishes itself from other amorous sentiments that seek a hug, a kiss, fooling around... Any one of those sentiments calls for me to enter a scene, that I do something with the beloved person. Tenderness, on the other hand, asks that I stay out. My entrance in the scene would ruin it, disturb the calm of the painting.

Tereza, asleep, provoked tenderness. Sleeping beings, even the most savage, become tender when they sleep. They turn into children. Maybe that's why Christian mythology has chosen as its supreme image of a divinity a sleeping babe. Who wouldn't like to have a God like that in their lap?

A sleeping child asks us to be no more than eyes. Any footstep, any word, any touch could awaken her. But the smile of the eyes is silent, leaving the scene untouched. Yes, hands touch the face... But how tender hands are different from hands that wish to possess. Tenderness wishes for nothing. It only wants to contemplate the scene. The tender kiss only brushes the lips. Tender hands are extensions of the eye. They touch to verify that their eyes aren't lying. Vincius de Morães said that a beautiful way: "What's left is this hand that touches before it takes, this fear of wounding by touch, this strong hand of a tame man..."

Poets, not knowing how to use a brush, use words to paint. I remember a poem by Cassiano Ricardo: "You and Your Portrait," in all ways like the painting by the Flemish master:

Why do I long for you, in the portrait, even though it's more recent?

And why does a simple portrait move me more than you do, if you yourself are here?

Maybe because the portrait, without the finery of words, has an air of remembrance.

Maybe because the portrait (exact though malicious) reveals something of a child(as, below the water, a coral in repose).

Maybe for the notion of absence that your portrait raises up between us (like a branch of hydrangea).

Maybe because your portrait, even when I turn aside, always looks right at me (amorously).

Maybe because your portrait looks more like you than you yourself do (ungratefully).

Maybe because, in the portrait, you are immobile (not breathing...).

Maybe because all portraits are palinodes.

The tender gaze wishes to be a painter, a photographer. The painting and the photograph eternalize the scene, crystalize the ephemeral. They are magical exorcisms against time. The tender gaze wishes that that moment be eternal. And thus its care, the soft voice, the hand that caresses, the slow movement: so the spell of the image does not break...

These were the thoughts that were playing with me, provoked by the woman with the candle. Satisfied, they left me alone. They went away. I felt sleepy again. And, for a brief moment between wakefulness and sleep, I had the impression that the wind would blow hard and extinguish the candle. Anyone who has the light of love does not need the light of a candle. I sank, then, again, into the dark of forgetfulness...

Violins Don't Grow Old

I wrote it a long time ago—a love story. Anyone who has read it has not forgotten it. Adélia gives the reason: "That which the memory loves is eternal." It's a story that was not made up. It happened, as touching as *Romeo and Juliet* and the story of Abelard and Heloise. All I did was register the occurrence. I need to tell it again for the benefit of those who didn't read it the first time, and in order to add a new ending, unexpected, that happened later.

The witness who told me of the event was a nephew, a medico-musician, a dear and handsome person. He was overdue for an appointment at my house, arriving three hours late, explaining that he had been at the wake of an uncle who had died of love at the age of 81. It seems that his old body could stand up to the intensity of his belated happiness. His muscles couldn't handle the young man that they were suddenly in charge of.

That love had arisen at the time when it was most pure: adolescence. But at the time there was another AIDS, called tuberculosis, which took pleasure in attacking beautiful people, the artists, the people in love—those were the high risk groups.

Tuberculosis, envious of the happiness of the two, lodged itself in the boy's lungs. He had to seek pure air high in the mountains at a sanatarium like the one Thomas Mann describes in his book *The Magic Mountain*.

Those who went to such places said good-bye with an "*adeus*" and a look of "never again." In the best hypothesis, many years would pass before they met again.

I can imagine the suffering of a young woman divided: the body, in that house, a soul in a far-away land! In the life of that girl, stupefied, the war lost... (Cecília Meireles).

More weighty was the prudent advice of her mother and father: to not trade a sure thing for something doubtful. A live businessman was worth more than a dead consumptive. And the same thing happened to her that happened with Firmina Dazza, who, hidden and from afar, went on loving Fiorento Ariza in the story by Gabriel García Márquez, *Love in a Time of Cholera*. She was obliged by her father to marry the doctor Urbino: don't trade a doctor for an office worker. She married him and stayed with him until, after 51 years, she was freed...

She married. He married. They never saw each other again. When he was 76 years old, he became a widower. When she was 76 (and he 79), she became a widow. And she learned that he was alive. Curiosity and longing were too strong. She went looking for him. They met. And all of a sudden, they were adolescent lovers again. They decided to get married. Their children objected. They—the children, all children—couldn't stand the idea that old people, too, have sex. Especially their parents. Old parents should be cute. They should know how to tell stories, should care for their grandchildren. But an old person in love is ridiculous. It doesn't work. There are more details in Simon de Beauvoir's book on old age. And there was also that story on the program *You Decide*. An old father, unhappy with his wife for his entire life, meets a woman and falls in love with her. The question: should he or should he not leave his wife to live with his new love? You decide... The public decision—the children, evidently: "No, he should not live with his new love..." The children always decide against their parents' love.

But in our story, the two oldsters gave their kids a solemn finger and went to live together in Poços de Caldas.[13] They lived a year of wonderful love, and he even started to write poetry and went back to the violin, which had been in a closet for more than 50 years because his wife didn't like violin music. He confessed to my nephew: "If God gives me two years of life with this women, my life will have been worthwhile..." And that's what God wanted. But his body wouldn't allow it. He died of love, just as Vinícius de Morães feared for himself.[14]

---

[13] A quaint town in Minas Gerais, Brazil.

[14] When the romantic bossa nova composer Vinicius de Morães (1913-1980), it was commonly said that he died of love.

I thought the story so beautiful that I turned it into a piece for a newspaper and gave it a title inspired by the Gospel: "...and the old shall fall in love anew."

Here begins the new ending to the story.

Tw weeks went by. It was ten o'clock at night. I was working in my office. The telephone rang. On the other end, the velvety voice of a woman.

"Is this Professor Rubem Alves?"

"Yes," I answered dryly. I am always dry on the telephone.

"I would like to thank you for the lovely piece in the newspaper that you wrote with the title, "...and the Old Shall Love Anew." You must have already guessed who's calling."

"No," I answered. Sometimes I'm quite the idiot. So she revealed herself.

"I am the widow."

It was the beginning of a delightful conversation of more than 40 minutes, long distance, in which she told me details I had not known. The fear that she'd had when he decided to have that violin fixed! She feared that his fingers were already too stiff...

Oh! What a fascinating metaphor for a sensitive psychoanalyst. Yes, yes! Not even violins grow too old, nor do fingers become impotent at producing music! And she went on talking, talking, reliving, smiling, crying—so much joy, so much longing, a whole eternity in a grain of sand... At the end, she made this marvelous observation:

"So that's it, Professor. At our age, we don't mess around much with sex. We live on tenderness!"

Here ends the lesson of the Gospel.

Maps

Once again I looked over Vermeer's painting. The name of it says almost nothing: *Woman in Blue Reading a Letter*. In fact, for those who only see what the eyes see, that's all that's there. A pregnant woman, standing, profile, a blue robe, reads a letter. Her lips are slightly apart, her face lit by a very subtle, almost imperceptible smile. Behind her is an enormous map of Europe and the coast of Africa that covers the whole wall.

Paintings are like dreams. Nothing in them is by chance. That map isn't there by accident. The painter put it there for some reason. Actually, its reflected light is what illuminates the brilliant light that shines on the letter.

What does the map say?

I don't know any woman who has ever allowed a map of that size to take up an entire wall of her house. pictures, plates and posters are more common decor. But that map isn't just a map. It doesn't say this in the painting. There are many things that painters don't manage to say. Things that they can only suggest in the hope that the sensitive observer will see what cannot be painted. The essential is invisible to the eyes. What is seen is nothing compared to what is imagined.

I imagined that her map was a gift of love. More precisely, of a love that was preparing to depart. For isn't that what the picture is saying—that the man she loves is a sailor who is far away, far away from home in a place undefined in that immense sea. Yes, he must have left on the next day. But he didn't want to go. He had to leave a piece of himself with the woman he loved. And, in fact, that's what he did. She was pregnant. That the painter can show. In the embrace of love, the man had said, "I remain inside you!"

But that wasn't enough for him. He wanted more. From his distance, he would always know where she was. But her? How would she know? That's why he thought of the map. He bought it and brought it to her. Oh, a strange gift, that one! He opened the map and his fingers went tracing routes, pointing out ports, marking times. Those would be the paths of his absence. So when she missed him, her pregnant fingers could caress that map as if it were his body. Many are the possible ritual eucharists: "This is my body!"

Happy is the language in which the word "*carta*" [a word in Portuguese meaning both *letter* and *map*, as in *cartography*] has two meanings. Until the *carta* arrives, she can console herself with the *carta*. When separation takes place, the spaces between lovers turn into maps. The Brazilian painter Wesley Duke Lee, some years ago, painted a work to which he gave the name *Cartografia Anímica*: the soul map. I liked the idea. And I imagined that the first maps were not made in the interest of scientific description and specialized abstraction. The first maps must have been instruments of love: signs on the bark of a tree indicating the place to meet. It's still like that today. We just use addresses and telephone numbers instead of signs on tree bark.

Maps, at their deepest level, are drawings we make for empty space to make separation less painful. When my mother died—she was 93—my brother told me that he was getting by with her absence by imagining her walking through sidereal space.

It is also said in *The Little Prince*. It was time for him to return to his little world. In the end, on his asteroid, there was a sheep and a rose waiting for him. But his new friend was suffering with the separation. He wanted the little prince to stay. The Little Prince had to explain:

> People have stars, and they aren't all the same. For some, the stars are guides. For others, they are no more than little lights. For the wise, they are problems to be solved. But all those stars are silent. You, however, will have stars like no one else... When you look to the sky at night, since I inhabit one of them, since on one of them I will be laughing, it will be as if all the stars are laughing. And you will have stars that know how to laugh! Your friends will be shocked to see you smiling when you look to the sky. And you will explain: Yes, the stars, they always make me laugh." And they will think you're crazy...

Maps are that way. I look at the vast spaces. I identify rivers, mountains, seas, cities. They don't tell me anything. But there are a few places that shine like stars. They are places where people I love live. Or places where I was happy, where I saw the beauty and experienced love. Each one has a map all its own. I imagine that, once the woman finishes reading the letter, she will turn to the map and smile while her hands go sliding over seas, continents, cities... Anyone who saw her in this state of ecstasy would conclude that she had gone mad. It's understandable. Only lovers know that maps easily turn into bodies. All that's needed is a good-bye...

Abelard and Heloise

It's a white marble tomb in the cemetery Père-La-Chaise in Paris. Under the protection of a canopy of open stonework, also of marble, they can be found in definitive form, modeled by memory, by night, by desire.

They lie side by side, in mortuary vestments, without touching each other, faces turned toward the sky, hands crossed over their chests, without desire. A sculptor sculpted them that way, conforming to the way religious tradition immobilized the dead. But if the choice were theirs, the sculpture would be something else—Rodin's *The Kiss*, their naked bodies in embrace. And the engraved words would be those of Drummond: "Love is the cousin of death, and the conqueror of death, even if it's slain (and it is slain) in every instance of love."

That's how the tomb of Abelard and Heloise is. They loved in a manner passionate and impossible, irremediably separated one from the other by life in the hope that death would join them eternally.

Love favored by fortune does not turn into literature or art. *Romeo and Juliet, Tristan and Isolde, the Bridges of Madison County, Love Story*—heart-touching love is wounded love. Octavio Paz says, "Things and words bleed from the same wound." But happy love isn't wounded. How, then, can words bleed from it? Happy love does not speak; it acts. If I write about Abelard and Heloise it's because their history is a wound in my own flesh. Heloise was 17, Abelard 38. Twenty-one years separated them. Love doesn't know time's abysms.

Abelard (1079-1120) was nicknamed "Wandering Bird." An effulgent intellectual, a central character in philosophical discussions in Paris, he was the cause of envy, hatred, and passion. Here's how Heloise described him in a letter to him:

> *What kings, what philosophers ever had renown equal to yours? What country, what city, what village never showed impatience to see you? You appear in public? Everyone rushes to see you. You go away? Everyone tries to follow you with avid eyes. What wife, virgin, hasn't burned for you in your absence and ignited in your presence? You possess, above all, two qualities capable of conquering all women: the charm of words and the beauty of voice. I don't believe that any other philosopher has possessed them to such high degree.*

Heloise, a young woman endowed with rare qualities of intelligence, lived in Paris in her uncle's house. He, wishing to give her the best education, hired Abelard as her intellectual tutor. But the philosophy lessons didn't last long. Soon the two were lost in love. And Abelard, a philosopher of incomparable logical rigor, turned into a poet. Heloise took care of his thoughts and his body and, from then on, according to his own confession, she found in him only "verses of love and nothing of the secrets of philosophy."

The uncle, discovering what was happening in his house, felt betrayed and became furious. He interrupted the "lessons" and prohibited them from seeing each other. To no avail. Distance doused nothing. It fanned the flames of love. Abelard himself comments: "The separation of bodies rose to the maximum the union of our hearts, and, because it wasn't quenched, our passion flared up more and more."

But Heloise got pregnant. Abelard decided to elope with her and take her somewhere far away. By night he got her from her uncle's house and took her to his sister's house in Palet, four hundred kilometers from Paris. And there the child of their love was born. They married secretly on July 30 of that year.

But for Heloise's uncle, the affair demanded revenge. So he planned the worst possible vengeance. He hired a band of thugs who invaded Abelard's house and castrated him. He thought that would put an end to the love. It was no use. They continued to love each other for the rest of their lives with the power of memory and longing—until death united them eternally. As in the film *The Bridges of Madison County*. Except that in the film, the instrument of castration wasn't the hatred of someone but the pious love of someone.

In 1142 Abelard died at the age of 63. Heloise, learning of his death, demanded possession of "her man" for herself. In fact, that was what Abelard had requested. "When I die," he wrote, "I ask you to have my body transported to the cemetery of your parish…" And Heloise requested that after she died, her body should be buried in her husband's tomb. Which happened 21 years later.

It is said that, on being taken to the tomb, when Abelard's coffin was opened, he opened his arms and embraced her. Others say that, to the contrary, it was Heloise who opened her arms to embrace him. It's possible. Perhaps Heloise's love had been more pure and intense. Abelard had known the love of many women and the love of philosophy. Heloise, on the other hand, knew only the love of Abelard. One of his biographies says: "For Heloise, there were only two events in her life: the day she knew she was loved by Abelard, and the day she lost him. Everything else disappears from her eyes in a deep night." Even today, after nine hundred years, lovers visit that tomb. Maybe to beseech God that they be eternally embraced, as in Rodin's *The Kiss*. Maybe to ask that we be given the happiness of living a love like that, but without living the pain. Love favored by fate, without literature, without fame, without anyone knowing. The illiterate happiness of "a homely little love," as Adélia Prado so lovingly baptized it, is enough for us. I am sure this is what Abelard and Heloise desired.

VII

Eternity

The Happiness of Parents

Once upon a time there lived an emperor, the father of several children, grandfather of my grandchildren. His children and grandchildren were more important than the administrative things of the empire and the war against enemies. He loved his children and grandchildren with all his heart.

Meanwhile, unfortunately, as happens with everyone stricken with love sickness, he suffered unceasingly the fear that Death would take one of them.

This took from him all the joy of living. During the day, he was tormented with worry. During the night, he was afflicted with insomnia. He never rested. His thought never stopped looking for ways to cheat Death.

His palace was full of doctors, laboratories, and medicines that battled Death in the trenches of infirmities. There were also guards all around, charged with combatting Death in the trenches of accidents.

But he knew that these precautions were not enough. Death is very clever. It attacks just when unexpected and in an unforeseen way.

So the emperor sent to have all the priests, prophets, fortunetellers, wizards, sorcerers, wisemen, gurus come from throughout his empire. He asked them to not only carry out appropriate magical rituals but also to write, in the pages of an enormous sacred book, made especially for this purpose from papyrus gathered on full moon nights in places where the gods lived, the formulas that would guarantee his children and grandchildren the long and happy lives that he desired. That was the only way he could live and die in peace.

Hearing the emperor's convocation, a wise old man can from a distant province. No one knew him. He lived in a faraway place, up in the mountains. The road he had to tread was long, and his legs were old and tired. He arrived late, after everyone else had performed their rituals and registered their wishes and departed.

The emperor was happy to be informed of the arrival of the saintly man, and he ordered his counselors to show him the sacred book. The wise old man carefully read the wishes that had been written there.

There were the wishes of simpletons who wished for the emperor's children and grandchildren protections of wealth, weapons, and armies.

There were prudent words that counseled moderation and healthy habits as the recipe for prolonging days.

There were the formulas of priests, who invoked the protection of the gods and the forces of good.

There were the spells of sorcerers and wizards who exorcized the forces of evil.

All these words brought the emperor great joy—and he believed that they would better protect those whom he loved.

After reading all that had been written, the wise old man took up a quill and recorded in the sacred book these words:

"The grandparents die. The parents die. The children die."

And he signed his name.

The emperor, upon reading these wishes, took it as a curse. Furious, he demanded that the wise old man explain himself, under penalty of being sent to prison for the rest of his days. Said the old man:

> Your Majesty, I do not know any formulas for impeding the arrival of Death. It comes, one way or another. I am only an old poet. My words have no power to exorcize it. What I can wish is that it come at the right time.
>
> The right time?
>
> What does a grandfather most wish? He wishes to die while seeing his children and grandchildren full of life and happiness.
>
> What does a parent most wish? He wishes to die while seeing his children full of life and happiness.
>
> Those who love die happy, and those who are loved continue to live. I have no magic words to keep Death from coming. But I offer you my wish that it come in the right order. I wish that Your Majesty die before your children and grandchildren.

That is why I called for Death in the order of happiness:

The grandparents die. The parents die. The children die.

The emperor smiled, took the wise old man's hands in his and kissed them.

The Egg

There were hundreds, maybe thousands, of all sizes and colors, some the size of a fingernail, others as big as a head. They followed me, wanting to eat me. They hated me and made weird noises, though they couldn't scream. Their numbers kept growing as they came closer and closer, eggs, thousands of eggs... It had all begun when I said, out loud that they weren't real eggs. A real egg:...

> *...doesn't fit inside itself, turgid with promise*
> *nature, dead, throbbing.*
> *Such a fragile white contains an occluded sun,*
> *what will live, waits.*

I asked them about the occluded sun, about the promises, and I asked them to let me listen to throbbing of dead nature in their chests. Full of hatred, they began to run after me. Fortunately, I came to a place where I could escape them, the eggs. I went in. It was cozy, familiar, the feeling of an old home, a church, so nice the stained glass, the signs, there was that certainty of being as it always been, the return to the old places of infancy. So I thought that there I would be able to hear what I wanted to hear, the stories about the tree that had been born of a sepulcher. Trees born from sepulchers? Of course. Anyone will know this if they've read the original story of Cinderella, where there was no fairy godmother, but there was a tree that the daughter planted in the tomb of her mother and watered it with her tears. The tree grew. Birds, its friends, lived in its branches. The poet T.S. Eliot knew this too. He asked himself:

> And the cadaver that you planted in your garden last year? Has it started to sprout yet? Will it produce flowers this year? Or has the unexpected frost disturbed its beds?

I confess that my garden is flowering. There are many bodies buried in it. I water it every day. There are always new sprouts rising from the ground. Its flowers always have such a lovely smell. Of course, of course, there are those that those who are rightfully afraid of the flowering of cadavers. That's why they put stones where they were planted, so they never come back, claiming that their return would bring sad memories.

But why would the dead returning to life have to bring sad memories? That gives me hope of me, after death, being reborn like a tree in whose branches birds land and that would be watered with the tears of people who love me. Oh! How I would like to be a tree. Yes, life is like that, bodies being planted whole. Love does not allow any body to be permanently unburied. Love calls for every body to be a seed that must be planted, an egg that must be hatched.

That's why the eggs were chasing me, because I had said that nothing would sprout from them. No pregnancy, just fat. And I noticed that they were piled up right over the place where a cadaver had been planted. They are put there so that there would be silence, so that no one would remember the dead since men no longer believe that trees sprout from tombs. They don't know how to tell stories, not even to themselves, nor even to their children. And today, just today, is the day on which the appearance of the sprout is celebrated, breaking the stone. In other places it's the beginning of spring. Ice still covers the fields. The trees, leafless, have an air of desolation and death. But all of a sudden, even in the middle of a hard frost, a fragile plant, with its own warmth, starts opening a way, breaking up through the sepulcher that covers it, to rise in triumph, colorful, unashamed, smiling, in the middle of the white snow.

The place was full, and I was happy when a man in priestly frock came up to the pulpit. I thought, "He's going to tell the story of the tree that was born from a tomb."

"The resurrection is the family united," he said. And his voice echoed through the empty space. I felt goosebumps. Yes, of course, a family united is a very good thing. Any fool knows that. But God would not need to die only to tell us that. The tree sprouts from the body even when the family is not united.

He continued: "The resurrection is social justice." Another chill went up my spine. Yes, of course, social justice is a very good thing. Any fool knows that. But the tree sprouts from the body even when there is no social justice.

Suddenly I understood that he was uttering these banalities because he, too, had forgotten the story. He didn't know how to talk about a tree sprouting from a body. In the end, what good was the tree? It was useless. Useless trees: we've already discussed them. From them no moral can be extracted, no warning, no words of prayer. They are only good for this happiness of the soul. A useless tree does not fill the stomach. It would be better to turn the story into the miracle of the multiplication of the loaves, pardon me, pardon me, I mean the story of the multiplication of the chocolate eggs...

At that moment the priest began to celebrate the eucharist, distributing chocolate hosts. As the faithful ate them, their faces turned into chocolate eggs. When the host was offered to me, I refused. Everyone looked at me, horrified at the sacrilege. In panic, driven by fear, in anger at the eggs that surrounded me, I heard my mouth shout the question that was pinched in my soul:

"And the body that you planted in the garden last year? Has it started to sprout? Could it be that it will produce blossoms this year?"

Everyone was paralyzed by my shout. There was a great silence. The eggs cracked, and from the cracks tears began to flow. And as they flowed, the faces recovered their human form. Everyone left, then, each one to plant a tree in their garden...

Cadavers

Sometimes the power of cadavers fascinates me. And I'm not the first. César Vallejo said of the body of a dead man that he "was full of worlds." Merleau-Ponty, for the same reason as Vallejo, considered them "sacred entities." Eliot, daring, asked:

And the cadaver you buried in your garden
last year
has it begun to sprout Might it produce blossoms
this year?

How crazy, to plant cadavers. To do this, you have to believe, as Adélia did, that

Never is anything dead.
What doesn't seem alive is decomposing.
What seems static waits.

It seems man always believes that, which would explain the custom of burying the dead with a thousand ministrations and watering the sowing with tears. Animals don't do that. Every burial is a planting. That's what Jesus believed, saying that the seed must die so that it can bear fruit.

What is said beside the dead is the beginning of the harvest. The dead make love with the living. Beside your dead body, Luiz Otávio, I would like to once again tell, in my own way, the story of the most handsome drowned man of the world, a story that Gabriel García Márquez heard, I don't know from which angel.

There was a village of fishermen somewhere at the end of the world, where things always happened the same way. The tedium and monotony settled into the bodies of men and women to the extent that all the light had fled from their eyes. No one expected either beauty or a smile from anyone's eyes. Everyone knew what everyone was going to say and what they were going to do. They knew the eternal repetition of the same vapidity, everyone secretly wishing the death of the others, freedom was a killer, the sea always the same, the sands, the stones, the boats, the fish, the living the dead, always the same...

One day a boy who eyeing the eternal monotony of the sea saw something different. It was far away. He didn't know what it was, but in a place like that, anything new was reason for nervousness. He shouted out, and everyone came running in the hope that they just might see something they could talk about. And there they were, on the beach, hoping the sea could bring them something. And it slowly came toward them, without hurry, until finally the sea dropped on the sand a dead man that no one knew, his denuded body dressed in nothing but seaweed, lichen, and green stuff from the sea.

Damned dead guy in total silence. Nothing could be said about him, an unknown stranger without a place, without a past, without a name...

But they had to do what they were supposed to do. Bodies must be buried. It was the custom in the village that women prepare the dead for burial. So they took him to a house and laid him eucharistically upon a table—*drink and eat for this is my body*—and great was the silence. Over a dead man with no name there was nothing to say. The women were inside the house, the men outside. And then one of the women said in a trembling voice, "If he had lived in our village, he would have had to lowered his head whenever he entered our houses, for he is very tall," to which everyone nodded imperceptibly.

But soon another woman spoke, asking how his voice might have been, if it had been like a breeze or like the roar of waves, and if in his mouth he'd had words which, once spoken, would make a woman pick a flower and put it in her hair. And all the women smiled, and some of them brushed their fingers through their hair, perhaps to feel for an invisible flower.

Great was the silence until the one who was cleaning the inert hands of the dead man asked what those hands might have done if they had built houses, had fought in battles, had navigated the seas, and if they had known how to caress the body of a woman. And then they heard a soft beating of wings, firebirds flying through the windows and penetrating their flesh.

And the men, scared, were jealous of a dead man who was able to make love with the women in a way that the men themselves didn't know. And they thought that they were too small, too timid, too ugly, and they wept over the gestures they had never made, the poems they had never written, and the women they had never loved.

The story ends with the men finally burying the dead.

But the village was never the same.

So, Luiz Otávio, pay attention! There are many wild birds beating their wings all around your body.

I Want a Yellow Ribbon...

Funeral homes cause me a double suffering. The first is the suffering of seeing the lifeless face of a person—any person. The second is the suffering of seeing the violence of the living against the defenseless dead: all funeral homes are, without exception, aesthetic violence.

In his essay on suicide, Albert Camus says that suicidal person prepares for the suicide like a work of art. Having not given life to life while alive, the suicide hopes that at least death will be beautiful, in all its horror.

How did Camus come to this conclusion? By going down the only path there is to the soul of a suicide: our own soul. Camus must have examined at length his own fantasies in the many times he planned his own death. It is inevitable that everyone who thinks and feels has done this, even though they never actually carried out their plans. By analogy I conclude that all of us who are going to die would also like for our last scene be as beautiful as a work of art. I learned that, in the Samurai tradition, the warrior, sensing the approach of death, leaves his word to the side and writes his last haiku—a minimal verse, an essential image that he wishes to see reflected in the eyes of those he's leaving behind. Each repetition would be a declaration of love and a confession.

If poets and artists had to deliver themselves to death, they should have to construct their last scene. Meanwhile, inexplicably, the living deliver their dearly beloved to the hands of strangers, death specialists who, having dealt with it so much, end up trivializing it and becoming insensitive to its terror and its beauty.

The doors of some Buddhist temples in the Orient are guarded by figures of horrifying monsters. I am told that the figures are put there to chase demons away. Not even demons can tolerate ugliness. I think the paraphernalia of burials are fabricated under the inspiration of a similar belief: it all has to be horrifying so that the demons flee and leave the dead alone.

Not even flowers, beautiful by nature, get away. Each bouquet arrangement is a coffin of flowers immobilized and tied down, their joy and beauty taken away, replaced by horrific purple ribbons and shopworn cliches written in golden letters.

Oh! How it would be different if the living decorated their last place with the same love that they decorate churches for weddings! People argue with me, saying that weddings should be happy and burials should be sad. I agree! But sadness can be beautiful! Sunsets: aren't they infinitely beautiful and infinitely sad? I would like my funeral parlor to be as beautiful as a sunset...

Let me suggest that, instead of arrangements of mummified flowers we send bromeliads, wild orchids, blooming azaleas, bonsais, seedlings of aromatic myrtle, and jasmine, all of which after the burial should be buried the same way in some place and turned into a garden. It's possible that the dead, seeing this gesture, would smile with happiness...

There's also the horror of funeral objects, those horrifying metal supports of intolerable bad taste on which the casket is laid to rest. And then there's the horror of the caskets themselves.

When I lived in the United States, someone I knew, someone relatively young, died. Over his rustic, unvarnished pine casket his wife laid a long sheet to which were sewn hundreds of red and yellow autumn leaves. I have never forgotten that.

National Geographic magazine (September 1994) published a very curious report on the art of constructing mortuaries in Ghana. They are made by artists in accordance with the wishes of people who are going to die: fish, boats, eagles, leopards—any image is a possible image for one's final resting place.

A good architect, planning a house, pays careful attention to the dreams of those who are going to live there. I think that funeral urns should be made with similar care. As for me, I would prefer that it be made of untreated wood, with no varnish, preferably smelling of pine, and of simple lines—the essential, as in haiku.

There's also the horror of the words that are said, "eternal rest," which always gives me gooseflesh of fear. "God called," as if he were an inhabitant in the grave who didn't know about the joys of this world. "He's better off this way…"

Better would be the words of poets, who know nothing of other worlds but know much about longing…

longing is the opposite of birth
longing is cleaning the room of a child who has died…

I'd like the living to feel the way suicides feel, that they were preparing their last scene like a work of art. What Manuel Bandeira said in his last poem is that which those who are going to die wish for their last act:

This is how I'd like my last poem
That it be eternally saying things simpler and less intentional
That it be burning with a sign without tears,
That it have the beauty of flowers without aroma,
The purity of the flame in which the clearest diamonds are consumed,
The passion of suicides who kill themselves without explanation.

And don't forget the truth that Noel Rosa said, with a smile:
When I die
I want neither weeping nor candle
I want a yellow ribbon
engraved with her name…

For Tom Jobim[15]

Dear Tom:

There are two kinds of sadness—sad sadness and happy sadness. Sad sadnesses are sadnesses for things that could have been but weren't. Happy sadnesses are sadnesses for things that could have been and were. And that's what I'm thinking with your death. I am happy sad. Sad because you went away, and happy because you lived. And I say to you what I judge to be the highest declaration of love that can be made: How good that you existed!"

"Hey! Hey!" the scared macho will say, "a declaration of love to a man..." I feel no shame whatsoever. Sônia Braga[16] said that you were the man that every woman would like to have, because you were masculine and feminine at the same time. I think she was right. And be-

---

[15] Tom Jobim (1927-1994) was Brazil's most well known composer, musician, and singer, one of the main progenitors of bossa nova in the 1960s.

[16] Film actress and singer renowned for her beauty.

cause you were feminine—that tender smile, that voice full of gentleness—I feel I have permission to love you with tenderness. I would like to be able to give you a hug. Tom, I think that today, the day you have returned to the mystery of the sea, Brazil is an immense *Pietà:* we are a mother with a dead son in our lap. We weep...

We weep a happy sad weeping—for there is one thing that not even death can do: it does not have the power to douse the music that you made. In truth, I am not even sure you made it. Music is a mysterious thing. I do not believe that we mortals have the power to make it. Music is eternal. It has always existed. It existed before the creation of the Universe. The holy author who wrote "In the beginning was the word," was, I believe, equivocating. What he wanted to say was, "In the beginning there was music..." It is to that which I give the name God.

I almost wrote something absurd, but I stopped myself in time. I was going to say "mystery and silence of the sea." But I remembered that silence exists only for us, who have common ears. In one of his most beautiful poems, Fernando Pessoa wrote:

...and the melody that hadn't been
if now I remember it,
makes me weep...

Music is the mysterious sea from which we are born. To say that a musician composes music is like saying that fish invented the sea. It wasn't music that germinated from you. It was you who germinated from music. Philosophers and ancient mystics held the wonderful theory that the Universe was created by God as the chorus and orchestra that played the melody that hadn't been—so that it was! I agree. Musicians aren't those who compose music. They are the ones who have the power to hear the melody that our mortal ears cannot hear.

You, Tom, played piano, and the beauty made us happy in body and soul. But you must have known that you yourself were the piano that the gods played for their own happiness. Because the gods envied what we feel when our body is touched by beauty and moves with the rhythm. The gods invented the piano and people like you as a ritual of sorcery in the hope that music would give them bodies like ours. Perhaps—an hypothesis to be considered by theologians—music attains its supreme beauty only when it is heard by mortal ears.

You know, Tom, I am here improvising on my keyboard, trying to make music with words. I'm working on an article that's been put away for a long time. I remembered it when I heard tell that your problem was "oedi...piano," as in "oedipal."[17] In Portuguese, it's a lovely play on words, mixing love and music. The name of the article file is "The Piano." I named it that because in it I kept ideas I had after seeing the film of the same title. I thought about writing a newspaper chronicle, but before long I gave up. Nothing I said could compare

---

[17] In Portuguese, *Edipiano*.

with that marvelous film in which the body of a woman and the keys of a piano are the same thing.

Before my eyes, that insuperable image appeared: the furious sea licking the smooth sand of the beach that the light transformed into a mirror that reflected a piano. There it was, in a single image, a summary of the cosmological myths: the struggle between the fury of chaos and the beauty of the body—the sea in struggle with the piano.

What a wonderful piano the girl from Ipanema must have been. Body and sea must know how to love...

This image made me remember an old poem that I memorized in school—one you probably learned, too—by Casimiro de Abreu, I believe:

> *I remember, I remember, I was small and was playing on the beach... The sea roared. And arching its proud back it shook the white foam at the serene sky. And I said to my mother at that moment: What a tough orchestra! What crazy fury! What could be greater than the ocean or stronger than the wind? My mother, smiling, looked at the sky and answered, "A being we don't see is greater than the sea we fear, and greater than the typhoon, my son. It's God!"*

My version is the same, different only at the end, Jobim. And I dedicate it to you, for if there is one person with the power to say the last thing that's been said, that person is you.

I remember, I remember, I was little and playing on the beach... The sea roared. And arching its proud back, it shook its white foam at the serene sky. And I said to my mother at that moment: What a tough orchestra! What crazy fury! What could be greater than the ocean? My mother smiled and looked at me and answered, "the piano..."

Well, Tom: I knew that's what you would say. With your piano you tamed the sea. Knowing that you have gone into the absolute sea, I have no fear of going after you. I will follow the sound of the piano...

The Final Agreement

I had put on the record player that record with poems by Vincius de Morães and Carlos Drummond de Andrade, an old record, a long-play endangered by the risk of making the needle jump. Fortunately, up until then, everything was smooth and nice, with no skips and no hiss, Vincius himself, in his voice hoarse with whiskey and smoke, was reciting the sonatas of separations and good-byes, of total love, of the eyes of his beloved. Finally, the last poem came, my favorite. "O Haver" ["Credit," as in bookkeeping]. Vinicius noticed that night was falling, so he tried to balance out what was done and, from that, what was left over. That's why all the strophes start with the same word, "*Resta...*" [There remains]. That's what was left over.

"There remains this capacity for tenderness, this perfect intimacy with silence..."

"There remains this urge to weep before beauty, this blind cholera in the face of injustice and misunderstanding..."

"There remains the incoercible ability to dream and that little indecipherable light to which poets sometimes take as hope..."

The last stanza began just then, and from the many times I've read it and other times I've heard it, I knew the words by heart, and I repeated them inside myself, anticipating the last, which would be the end, knowing that everything that is beautiful must end.

Sunset is beautiful because its colors are ephemeral. In a few minutes they no longer exist. If the sonata were a song without end, it is certain that its place would be among the Devil's instruments of torture in Hell.

Even the kiss...what lover can tolerate a kiss that never ends?

The poem also had to die to be perfect to be beautiful and for me to miss it after it's over. Everything that becomes perfect asks to die. After the death of the poem comes silence and emptiness. Something else is born in its place: longing. Longing blooms only in absence.

It is in longing that gods are born. They exist so that which was loved and lost can return, that life be like the record that can be played as many times as you wish. The gods—I have no love for them in themselves. I love them only for their power to bring things back so that the embrace can be repeated. The gods are not divine. Re-encountering is divine.

Vinicius's voice announces the end. He speaks more softly.

> *There remains this daily dialog with death,*
> *this fascination with the moment to come,*
> *when, emotions stirred,*
> *she will come to me to open the door to an old lover...*

And I, in my head, automatically thought ahead, reciting silently the last verse: "...without knowing that it's my newest lover."

And it was then, at that last moment, the unforeseen happened: the needle jumped back, maybe for having thought the poem so beautiful that it refused to be an accomplice to its end, did not accept its death. And there was the dead voice of Vinicius repeating words without meaning: "without knowing it's my newest... without knowing it's my newest...without knowing it's my newest..."

I got up and went over to the record player, and I carried out the murder: I smoothly pushed the arm with my finger, and helped the beauty die. I helped to make it perfect. It thanked me, said what it had to say: "...without knowing it's my newest lover...." After that, silence.

I thought that had to be a parable of life, life as a work of art, a sonata, a poem, a dance. In that first moment when the composer or poet or dancer prepares his or her opus, the last moment is already in gestation. It is quite possible that the last verse of the poem had been the first that Vinicius wrote. Life is a weaving like the web of a spider: they always begin at the end. When life begins at its end it is always beautiful for being colored with the colors of twilight.

No, I do not believe that biological life should be preserved at any price.

"For all things there is a certain moment. There is the time to be born and the time to die." (Ecclesiastes 3:1-2)

Life isn't a biological thing. Life is an aesthetic entity. Once the possibility of feeling joy before beauty is dead, life as God gave it to us also dies—even if the paraphernalia of the doctors go on emitting their beeps and making zig-zags on the video.

Life is like that opus. It needs to end.

Death is the last agreement that says: it is complete. Everything that is complete wishes to die.

Odyssey

There it was, a cocoon, hanging on the front door. Immobile. I remember a verse by Adélia: "Nothing is ever dead. What seems to be still, waits." In the cocoon, something was waiting.

It must have been one of those disgusting caterpillars that had been eating my plants a few days before. Asking for pardon, I had smashed some that were crawling on the ground. I had to to defend my plants.

I imagine the whole thing started when in a silent voice one of them was told, "The time to stop eating has come. Prepare to die. Begin to construct your shroud." And then, without protest, she abandoned her green leaves, crawled to someplace firm where she could fix her casket, and began to build, with material taken from her own body, that perfect box that now contains her, hanging on the front door. I knew that inside magical transformations were underway. What looked like a tomb was actually a uterus.

Days later the cocoon was still there. Empty. Just the shell. What had once crawled had gained wings. The caterpillar had turned into a butterfly. I was happy to think that my plants had contributed to that amazing event.

It was an event so amazing that Greek myth took the butterfly as a symbol of the soul. The soul is a butterfly. It does not submit to the laws that rule the common life of creatures who live in time, those who are born, grow, mature, die, and rot. The soul, like the butterfly, is a being of resurrections.

Zarathustra said, "Only where there are graves are there resurrections."

For there to be resurrections, there must first be deaths. If a caterpillar doesn't die, it remains a caterpillar. But if it dies, it becomes a butterfly. "Die and transform," Goethe said.

There is also, in life, a moment when a voice tells us that the time has come to die. No, please, don't misunderstand me. I am not referring to physical death. I refer to a voice that tells us that the time has come for a great transformation: we must abandon that which we always were so we can turn into something else. The time to become young again.

Zarathustra spent ten years alone high on a mountain. Now he was returning—after a great transformation. An old man who lived in the forest recognized him and said to him, "This walker is no stranger to me. Many years ago he passed by here. But he has changed. Back then, you took your ashes to the mountain. Now you take your fire to the valley? Do you not fear being punished as an incendiary? Yes, Zarathustra has changed. Zarathustra has turned into a child."

A caterpillar becomes a butterfly, an old man turns into a child... Time completes its cycle, returns to its beginning. Thus is the soul's time, a carrousel, turning, always coming back to the beginning, the "eternal return." T.S. Eliot was right when he said that "The end of all our explorations is to arrive at the place we came from and to then know it for the first time."

And that was the feeling of Joseph Knecht, the Magister Ludi Josephus III, the main character of that wonderful book by Hermann Hesse, *The Glass Bead Game*. At the end of his academic career, in the flash of his "twilight shine," when he was able to dedicate himself to the pleasure of the spirit's highest joys, he discovered that the end would bring him to his beginnings. He wanted to go back to teaching children. And the younger and less ruined they were by diseducation, the greater his pleasure would be.

Barthes felt the same when he got old. He said that he forgot the age of his body in order to become a contemporary of his students' young bodies. "Once in a while I must be reborn," he said, "to make myself younger than I am, to enter a *vita nuova*."

It is the old who are are closer to children. "Oh winter, infancy of the year! O infancy, the winter of life!" said Miguel de Unamuno. He understood the solidarity between old age and infancy: "The great silences of a child's soul! The great silences of an ancient's soul!"

We are used to seeing time represented as an old man with a huge white beard. Heraclitus, a philosopher of time, river, and fire, disagreed: "Time is a child playing; it is the reign of a child." But maybe the two are right: the old man and the child play together."

Of all the science fiction films I've seen, only one made me wiser: *2001–A Space Odyssey*. An odyssey is a long trip home. Ulysses sailing the seas. But now, the seas having been conquered, space remains unexplored. The home changes place. Men of science hear a voice coming from the immensity, telling them that home is on a distant planet, Jupiter. So they prepare an "odyssey," They launch a starship, headed for home. After overcoming dangers, the astronaut approaches his destination. But, oh! He is not prepared for that which awaits, a nightmarish turmoil of dizzying, confusing shapes in psychedelic colors: the trip through cosmic space turns into an odyssey through the spaces of the soul.

He gets there. His clear visor fills the screen. It is I who am looking through it. I am the astronaut. The air is cloudy, leafy green, like a dream. But what a plain place: the kitchen of a common house where a man, his back to us, eats his breakfast. The silence is absolute. All of a sudden the man turns to look at the visitor—and his face is the astronaut's! A trip so long to meet himself. A jerky movement, and the man knocks over a crystal cup. It falls and breaks. I remember the Holy Scripture: "Sooner would the cup of silver break…" The crystal cup shatters, and the scene is transformed. Now the astronaut, terribly old, is on his deathbed. He contemplates the starry heavens through which he has navigated his whole life. And then he sees something he had never seen before. Between suns and planets, a fetus, floating, contemplating the mysteries and beauty of the universe through enormous eyes...

I paraphrase Eliot: the end of our long adult explorations will be to finally arrive at our point of departure, the child, that we may then know ourselves for the first time...

Rio

We gather flowers,
We lightly wash
Our hands
In the calm rivers,
That we may learn
Calm, too...
Ricardo Reis, *Odes*, p.15

Adélia Prado said that God, one in a while, punishes her. He takes away her poetry. She looks at a rock, and sees only the rock itself.

Poetry is born from the work of powerful eyesight that casts its magic light on things, turning them to glass. They might become transparent, letting us see what's behind them (as is the case of Christ in Salvador Dalí's *The Last Supper*), or they might turn into mirrors, showing reflected images of absent things, as in the case of Lewis Carroll, making Alice go through the looking glass and entering a world of spectacular images. Escher, the Dutch artist, made a beautiful engraving like that. That's the way the entities are that poets make with their poems: dreams and dream-catchers.

Bachelard looked at the flame of a candle that was going out. A dream object. But he saw more than that. He saw a sun dying. He kept looking, and the dying sun turned into something else. "A damp, liquid, ardent flame slipping to the heights, to the sky, like a vertical stream."

At noon the sky is a dome of blue agate, immobile and eternal. At dusk, the stone liquifies, the blue turns to yellow, green, pink, orange, purple until it disappears into the black abyss of night's cascade.

Everything that is solid liquifies at dusk. "No one can enter the same river twice," said Heraclitus. The Being of the river is its permanent Unbeing. I can well imagine that this was the sadness that led Narcissus to his death: the beauty of his face was liquid. It couldn't be had. It slipped away and disappeared whenever his hands tried to grab it. Dusk and the river inform us that we have nothing. It is impossible to add up. We can only subtract down... We are—not accidentally but metaphysically, inescapably—mourners. "The river is a traveler of itself, it is its own trip," said Heládio Brito in one of his poems. The river is a permanent self-realizer, distant from what it is near. All is leave-taking. "Every dock is a longing for stone," said Álvaro de Campos. The dock is the place where the solid sinks into the liquid. What remains is empty space...

Wondering, as a psychoanalyst, about the philosophy of Parmenides, and not as a philosopher because philosophers are prohibited from wonder, I imagine that his thought was born under the light of noon, when everything seems stopped, time suspended, Being looking like something immobile and eternal. Heraclitus, meanwhile, a philosopher of fire and river, certainly loved to let his thoughts be taken away by the waters of the river, especially when the colors of the dying sun were reflecting in it. He may well have repeated, like a Taoist poet, the short verse that sums it all up: "The sound of water says what I think." What great friends Heraclitus and Monet would have been. Monet spent the whole day painting painting after painting of the same pile of hay. Pardon me, my slip-up...If he heard me say "the same" pile of hay, he would correct me to tell me that light is a river that runs, and that each shift of light on the pile of hay turns it into something else. Just as you can't step into the same river twice, you can't paint the same object twice. All is liquid and...uncertain.

In his book *Tao: The Watercourse Way*, Alan Watts writes, "Especially to the extent that you go on getting old, it becomes more and more evident that things don't possess substance, since time seems to pass ever faster so that we become conscious of the liquidness of solids. People and things come to look like reflections and ephemeral ripples on the surface of water."

Guimarães Rosa wrote one of the most mysterious stories I have ever read: "The Third Bank of the River." A mysterious story is one that remains in one's thoughts, like an unsolved enigma. It's the story of a father who, at a certain time in his life, decided to trade *terra firma* how, wife, and children for the waters of the river. He had a canoe made of good wood that would last at least 30 years. Indifferent to the extreme vociferations of his wife, and with no explanation whatsoever, he got the canoe, said good-bye with his eyes, and pushed off into the river, never to return. No, he didn't leave to go somewhere else. He did not disappear. Usually a canoe and a river are used to go somewhere. He used the canoe and the river to go nowhere, just to be on the river, navigating. "The Third Bank of the River"–strange title because rivers have only two banks. What would the third bank be? Time? Maybe that was it: the third bank of the river is the sands and foams that the river leaves in our heads in the form of words and poems. *Tempus fugit*. "It isn't eternal, it's a flame"–is all the river says.

Guimarães Rosa made a strange confession. He said that he would like to be a crocodile,

> because I love big rivers, for they are as deep as the souls of men. On the surface they are very lively and clear, but down deep they are tranquil and dark like the sufferings of man. I love one more thing about our big rivers: their eternity. Yes, river is a magic word for conjugating eternity...

It's curious that in the river, the ephemeral and the eternal are together...

Vaseduva, the boatman, was a disciple of the river all his life. And he learned so much that he could even give lessons to Siddhartha: "The river taught me to listen," Vaseduva said to Siddhartha... "The river knows all things. From it all things are learned. The voices of all living creatures can be heard in its voice." And so they sat together, on the tree trunk as night fell. They listened to the water in silence, water that for them wasn't just water but the voice of life, the voice of Being, of eternal Transformation...

Gratitude

The translator would like to thank editors Ralph Hunter Cheney and Denise Dembinski for applying their critical eyes to every inch of this book. Thanks are also due Dr. Ana Lessa-Schmidt for consultation on translation. The publisher thanks Raquel Alves and the Instituto Rubem Alves for permission to translate and publish this work.

Rubem Alves

Rubem Alves (1933-2014) was a Brazilian theologian, philosopher, educator, and psychoanalyst. He was the author of more than 40 books of essays, fiction, children's literature, and newspaper columns. His doctoral dissertation at Princeton Theological Seminary formalized the term liberation theology. He taught philosophy at the State University of Campinas, Brazil. More information is available at wikipedia and rubemalves.com.br.

THE TRANSLATOR

Glenn Alan Cheney is a writer, translator, and managing editor of New London Librarium. He has translated several books by Rubem Alves and contributed translations to *Ex Cathedra: Stories by Machado de Assis* and *Trio in A-minor: Stories by Machado de Assis*. He has written more than 35 books on such disparate topics as the Pilgrims of Plymouth, Chernobyl, nuns, Brazil's Quilombo dos Palmares, the Estrada Real, Amazonia, Abraham Lincoln, Mohandas Gandhi, cats, bees, death and burial, incarceration, eschatology, and nuclear issues.

www.ingramcontent.com/pod-product-compliance
Lightning Source LLC
Chambersburg PA
CBHW030331230426
43661CB00032B/1370/J